AMERICA'S FIRST BLACK NAVY SEAL

BILL GOINES, FORGED THROUGH ADVERSITY

RODNEY E. WALKER

America's First Black Navy SEAL

William Goines–Forged Through Adversity

UDT21–SEAL TEAM

ISBN: 979-8-218-98798-5

Cover Designer: Rose Miller

Format Designer: Dawn Baca

Created with Vellum

DEDICATION

To my mother: Betty Jean Johnson [Walker]
Thank you mom for diligently teaching me how to read
and then encouraging me to write.

CONTENTS

FOREWORD

This book is about the first black Navy SEAL.

Momentous?

Yes, for various reasons.

Foremost, because Bill Goines was chosen to be among the original 50 men selected from the ranks of Underwater Demolition Team 21 to become a "Plankowner" with the first Navy SEALs. He was not chosen because of the color of his skin, but for significant prowess and leadership as a U.S. Navy "Frogman" and SEAL. He was, in fact, an accomplished and superior Underwater Demolition Team (UDT) and SEAL Team operator.

Bill Goines is sadly now deceased, and his friend Rodney Walker has made it his passion to honor Bill's lifetime and legacy by sharing this fabulous story. Fortunately, Rodney was able to conduct numerous interviews with Bill before he passed.

Bill was raised in segregated communities in Dayton and Lockland, Ohio. During his childhood and emerging years, the country was deeply segregated. His mother and father were proud and loving parents, but, even at an early age, he was exposed to negative racial attitudes. Schools were not integrated, and 'coloreds' were not allowed in most school or community swimming pools.

But Bill had a goal. He taught himself to swim, and based on watching a movie about Navy Frogmen he was inspired to decide what he wanted to become.

In 1955, Bill joined the Navy, which also was dealing with integration and segregation issues. Through several assignments, and in spite of several setbacks, he endured until finally being selected to begin Basic UDT training—to finally attain his goal of becoming a Navy Frogman. He completed this arduous training which unfolds as a compelling story of steadfastness and fortitude, that led him to a lifetime of excitement, adventure, and danger.

There is no doubt that Bill Goines was special. Regardless of his positive demeanor and striking good looks, as a black man he still experienced racism. With exceptional determination he ended up in a community of men that largely didn't judge a person by the color of their skin, but rather by how reliable and capable they were at doing their essential "no- fail" jobs.

Bill and I served on SEAL Team TWO at the same time. And, although I knew him well in the Team and beyond, we never deployed together. We were all deploying to Vietnam at various stages during this period and many men in the Team didn't often cross paths. Indeed, Bill had multiple deployments to Vietnam where his performance was exceptional.

Eventually he was promoted to the rank of Master Chief Petty Officer; the highest rank an enlisted Sailor can attain in the Navy. He was later selected to become the Command Master Chief at Naval Special Warfare Group TWO, which made him the senior enlisted advisor to the Group Commander and senior SEAL among all Atlantic Fleet Navy SEALs.

He accomplished beyond measure the capability to obviate the color spectrum in the Teams and, perhaps to some degree, the Navy and military in general.

Bill retired from the Navy in 1987 after 32 years of service. He was a recipient of the Bronze Star Medal with Combat "V", Navy Commendation Medal with Combat "V", Meritorious Service Medal, Combat Action Ribbon, and Presidential Unit Citation among other awards.

He died on 10 June 2024 in Norfolk, Virginia at the age of 87 years.

Commander (SEAL) Tom Hawkins, USN, Retired
Purveyor of SEAL history and friend of Bill Goines

1

WHY DID THEY HATE US?

There were no public swimming pools for 'coloreds' where I grew up. I had to teach myself how to swim. I always waited at the edge of the creek to make sure there wasn't an undercurrent before jumping in, because I had a buddy who wasn't careful and drowned there. He got snagged underwater on a fallen tree branch; we were about nine years old at the time. But I found my own rhythm moving my hands, feet, legs—keeping my head above that murky, brown water. I loved it, and of course, it all worked later to my advantage as a U.S. Navy SEAL.

I was born in Dayton, Ohio as William Harvey Goines. I grew up in a segregated community where my mother stayed home and took care of the kids—that was a full-time job for her. And my father worked in a Buick auto dealership but was fired from some good positions because of racial attitudes at the time. He was very fair-skinned and also a very proud black man. This sometimes created confusion with others. Once when my mother, who had darker skin, brought lunch to my father at his workplace, his boss got angry with him for having his "maid" deliver his lunch. When dad set him straight, proudly identifying her as his wife and identifying himself as black, he lost his position.

Often the car dealer would send him to Detroit to pick up cars because back in those days they didn't have great big, long vans where you could put eight or nine cars on a trailer. They would put six or seven guys in a big Buick and have them drive to Detroit, then five of the guys would each pick up a new car and drive it back to the dealership in Cincinnati.

My father also ran a pool parlor after work to subsidize his salary, straining to provide for us three children. He took good care of family as well as he could, and he and I got along great. He later moved us all to Lockland, Ohio where we could be closer to our grandparents who had a big house.

In my youth I was as strong as an ox because I had to work like one. Since my grandfather didn't have a horse to plough his farm I was put to good use cutting into that hard ground, turning over old crop stubble with a push plough. I'd push that plough over ten miles to get 1 acre ready for planting and usually felt it in my abs, lower back, shoulders, hamstrings and thighs the following day. But it was good work and good conditioning. I soon developed a reputation for being the quiet and strong guy whom you probably didn't want to mess around with.

We had two schools in the city—one black, one white. We were West Lockland, and they were East Lockland, but they had a big, nice swimming pool and gym while our school had to use their throwaway stuff—uniform hand-me-downs and things like that. We had no swimming pool, and we surely weren't allowed to use their swimming pool. Despite the fact that there was a nice public swimming pool in the city, no coloreds were allowed in it—period!

We could go way across town and use a public swimming pool which allowed blacks in on a limited schedule, but after we left the whites always felt they had to drain it, clean it and refill it with fresh water.

Why did they hate us?

We never really interacted with whites except for the times when I was younger we'd get into mini-BB-gun wars. We'd be on one side, and they'd be on the other and we'd just shoot at each other—I suppose one of us could have put someone's eye out. But when they were forced to integrate public services years later, members of the community drained the pool and filled it with rocks and boulders so that no one couldn't use it.

Though the whole community was segregated I wouldn't call my school a "segregated" school—we were an "all black" school. We were fully integrated with blacks—that's how we saw it. And we had good teachers who wouldn't put up with anything. Back in those days if the teacher told my father or mother that I was acting up, they'd believe the teacher; so naturally, we did as we were told.

But one day I had a woodshop teacher who wasn't around, and I did something stupid; I was either a freshman or a sophomore and I got lazy while operating a planer to smooth the surface of a board I was cutting for a table project. I was using a little block to support the wood piece, and I just zipped that thing through the planer and my fingers went in too far.

Those blades were so sharp that when I was badly cut I didn't even realize it. When some guy noticed that I was bleeding pretty bad we discovered that the top of my index finger had been cut off just beneath the joint. We went looking around for the missing limb and they found it up on the ceiling above us. We didn't think about having it stitched back on, and my concern was more about saving the rest of my finger. When they took me to the nurse, she passed out; I guess she might not have had much experience beyond treating tummy aches and fevers.

Eventually they were able to stop the bleeding and called my father, so the two of us walked to a doctor in Wyoming, Ohio about three or four miles away. That woodshop teacher didn't like me after that incident because he had been walking around the office flirting with young women when he should have been watching us.

Despite missing a part of my finger, I was able to make the basketball team. The school actually qualified for the state championships in 1953 and 1954; but I was too young for the team. By the next championships in '55 I had already graduated—so I never was able to share in that glory, but our team was the first African American high school in the nation to win a cross-racial state championship.

As a matter of fact, they were inducted into the Smithsonian National Museum of African American History and Culture in D.C. Our Assistant principal and coach, Joseph Martin, was the first African American to be appointed to an NBA assistant coaching position. He was hired by the Cincinnati Royals. So, even with all those many things against us, we knew we could be as good as anyone else.

As for me, I already knew what my career was going to be. I had seen an underwater commando movie about Frogmen starring Richard Widmark. I don't think there were any blacks in the movie, but when I saw it, my fate was sealed right there. Just watching those guys on their demolition runs, planting explosives to blow up underwater barriers for landing crafts to get through, I knew what I was going to do with the rest of my life. But first I'd have to go through the Navy to enroll for the Underwater demolition Teams (UDTs). I had no interest in going to college—I don't think my father and mother could have afforded it anyway.

Back then there weren't a lot of positions opened for blacks in the Navy. I had a buddy in the Army who tried to warn me that they would probably try to get me to shine officers' boots and things like that.

"I told you, the Navy ain't looking for you to be nothin'

but a shoe shiner. What else do you think they want to do with coloreds? You need to be ready for that reality."

"I've got my own plans, man, and that's not me. I know what I want and I'm going to make a way to get it."

I refused to be discouraged. I knew that if I started down the path of self-doubt, failure would probably become a self-fulfilling prophecy. I clung to the encouragement from one of the math teachers, Gus Giovanni, a strict disciplinarian who mentored many of us boys on how to rebound from racial prejudice by seeing it as a solvable mathematical equation. He was very effective with children. His young daughter, Nikki Giovanni, would later become a world-renowned poet. My sister, Beverly, and the then quiet and shy Nikki grew close. In time, Nikki's success would become a real boost for the African American community in the late 1960s and thereafter (she went on to be a Distinguished Professor at the Virginia Polytechnic Institute and State University [Virginia Tech] using her literary talents in the English department).

But the Navy in the 1950s didn't have a reputation for steering blacks in the direction of what we perceived as success. They guided us into taking steward classifications to serve officers and everybody knew it (U.S. Navy Stewardmates served food and did house cleaning chores for officers). But I didn't care. I was signing up for UDT to be a frogman and I left for the Navy right after graduating from high school to get what was mine.

2

NAVAL BASE TRAINING

"Ain't no use a going' home"
"AIN'T NO USE IN GOIN' HOME!"
"Jodie's got your gal and gone"
"JODIE'S GOT YOUR GAL AND GONE!"
"Ain't no use in going' back"
"AIN'T NO USE IN GOIN' BACK!"
"Jodie stole your Cadillac!"
"JODIE STOLE YOUR CADILLAC!"
"Left-right, left-right, left-right left!"
"LEFT-RIGHT, LEFT-RIGHT, LEFT-RIGHT LEFT"
"Left-right, right, right-left"
"LEFT-RIGHT, RIGHT, RIGHT-LEFT!"
(Double-time marching cadence)

I arrived at the Bainbridge Naval training center in Port Deposit, Maryland, on August 29, 1955. This place was huge. They had us learning shipboard duties on a 200-foot vessel built on dry land. I think ours was one of the last sessions for new recruits before they permanently closed it down. It had already been closed down after World War II but reactivated in 1951 because of the Korean Conflict.

The first two weeks were supposed to be the hardest for physical training. We had to pass the Third-Class Swim Test with a deep-water jump, a 50-yard swim and a five minute float. Then we ran an obstacle course for a mock shipboard emergency. The instructor told us if we had to abandon ship, the best way was to go down a cargo net and step into a lifeboat—we were never supposed to dive overboard. The next best way was to pencil-dive; so, we practiced folding our arms over the lifejacket and jumping with our legs straight together.

Then we learned all the other basic things like knot tying and how to march to a heel-beat. How to carry weapons was something the commander taught, and then they went over the Uniform Code of Military Justice (UCMJ) which was like the Bible for us. I was relieved to see how, on several levels, fairness was intentionally reinforced through all military court proceedings—even more so than in the civilian sector. I learned the day before I entered boot camp about, Emmet Till, a colored boy in Mississippi who couldn't have been more than five years younger than I, was kidnapped and murdered. It was unbelievable that something like that could happen to a youth—and there clearly was no equal justice in the courts after they pulled his bloated body out of the Tallahatchie River.

Back to the Navy, we got through emergency activities like carrying sandbags, wearing an oxygen mask and throwing life rings into the water by working in groups of three–they were also trying to teach us teamwork. And, of course, we had to learn all the jargon.

"All hands": The call for everyone
"Aye Aye": I understand and will obey
"Best Bower": The largest anchor
"Blue Jacket": A Navy enlisted person
"Bug Juice": Insect repellant, or a flavored drink
"Companionway": Interior Stairway
"Dog Watch": Split watch between the hours of four and six, and six to eight
"Gig": A commander's personal boat
"Old man": A commanding officer

After duty hours we had time to mix it up and compete against each other in sports. Since the 1952 Olympics, Navy athletes were playing more and more on U.S. national teams, so I decided to try my luck and get involved in a little competitive boxing. I was pretty good at bobbin' and weavin'—I won two bouts. I got my experience from street fighting and was doing exceptionally well until someone outboxed me. When *that* guy hit me he sent me flying into the third seating row. After that, I knew my competitive boxing days were over—but no matter how good you are there will always be someone better, even Mohammed Ali learned that when he went up against Joe Frazier.

At about the fifth week all the recruits who hadn't washed out were scheduled to meet with Navy career mentors to get matched for a job classification. Some went on to technical schools like ship carpentry, metal molding, wire rigging, radio operating, and stewarding, but there was something going on with UDT training. Even though I had been promised that I could join UDT after boot-camp, they stopped the training that year. They were now talking about getting rid of UDT since the Korean War was well over and the whole purpose of UDT was to prepare beaches for landings. They didn't think they would need it anymore.

But I felt they had just messed me over. Now they were asking me what ship I wanted for duty, but I had no thoughts about any ship. Before I let the guy begin to coach me into any stewardship classification, I said I'd be interested in radio school and I haggled to be assigned to the USS Cambria. I didn't know it then but, providentially perhaps, it had been a transport ship for UDT operations at Okinawa and Leyte during World War II. She had at least two 40 mm gun mounts, and eighteen single 20 mm gun mounts; so before duty onboard the ship I had to complete a one-week training session at Gunnery School in Dam Neck, Virginia. After a few surprising disappointments there, my duty on the Cambria would become a blessing in disguise.

At boot camp racial relations had lightened up a little, so I went to Dam Neck with a white buddy who graduated with me. Excited to see the big city, we decided to go into Norfolk which was bustling at the time. Everybody was going there. But when we were leaving the quarterdeck the officer in charge called us over. He had been looking at me in a funny way:

"Y'all need to remember what's going on, on the outside. You're not in New York, or Chicago. When you leave this base you'll be entering a racially segregated area—this is the South. There are places where you won't be able to enter together."

We acted like we already knew what was going on and would figure it out as we went along. So, we stepped on the bus and rode all the way to Norfolk. Things seemed fine until we walked into a restaurant. You could feel a little change in the atmosphere when we stepped in. The host there casually glanced at us and sauntered over with a sense of urgency

"Nu, uh, you can stay (talking to my buddy in a paternal tone) but *he's* got to go."

This happened twice. Soon after that the shock began to take effect: to see all of the "No Coloreds Allowed" signs and even the "Dogs and Sailors keep off the grass" signs made things loud and clear. I remembered thinking back in Lockland we all just knew there were certain areas where we couldn't go—no need for signs everywhere. But this was in your face! When we were walking down Granby Street I noticed a big sign advertising the U.S. Navy at the YMCA. After hearing all the loud voices inside I said to myself, I guess they're having a good time there and I know I can get in because I'm in uniform—my buddy was right behind me. As soon as I walked in all I could see was Caucasians and Filipinos—Filipinos could go anywhere they wanted. I went over to the desk to talk with a guy in charge and I asked if it was okay for me to be in there:

"Hell no! We got a place across town called the Hunton YMCA, all set up for coloreds."

We were in a *Jim Crow* racist "Twilight Zone" and my buddy became scared, which seemed a little odd to me. If only he had been back in Lockland when a property owner released his two Great Danes on me because I had ventured too close to his white neighborhood, then he would know what being scared was about—I had been picking berries to sell and found myself on the wrong side of the tracks. But now in Norfolk, we both felt we had seen enough of life outside of the base, so we decided to make our own tracks and got on the bus to go back.

After gunnery school my duty on the USS Cambria turned into a blessing because I was only on it two months before a uniformed official came on board and said they needed three seamen to go to shore duty; which was unheard of for seamen. They said they needed two to go to Malta and one to Argentia, Canada. None of us knew where any of those places were, but I was lucky to choose Malta because Argentia was under snow 8-9 months out of the year and Malta was a paradise in the Mediterranean Sea.

Those Sapphire blue skies and clear waters of Valletta, the capital, made it a real tourist attraction. I sometimes felt more as if I were on vacation than reporting for duty on a British Air Base. When they learned that I could type, I was offered a "cushy" office job working in aviation electronics. The whole island seemed to be in a cooling down phase because four months before I got there the British were trying to capture the Suez Canal. As far as the eye could see there were these British Canberra bombers that would take off, one after another. Unfortunatly, we weren't allowed to take pictures of the bombers—we couldn't even mail anything out during that period.

The local people liked Americans; and maybe it was because the British treated the locals like slaves. I noticed how they talked about them and how they were unashamed about their attitude towards them—it was all too familiar to me. But there were plenty of ladies, bars, and good food. The Americans could date the British women of the Royal Naval Service (WRNS), generally called WRENS, and also the Maltese women.

We all lived in huts and sometimes had to come up with ways of entertaining ourselves. Off-duty, I earned money on the side running a movie house and on Sundays, a buddy and I regularly took a boat from the main island to attend church on a smaller island; you could still see the effects of World War II everywhere. One church, called the Mosta cathedral, was where a German bomb had fallen through the ceiling during a service. The bomb never exploded so they disarmed it and left its shell there on display stuck in the floor. They considered it a miracle.

Then the lucky break came. After spending ten months on shore duty, they asked me again if I was still interested in UDT replacement training; they were bringing it back to life. I responded in the affirmative, so they said we had to get moving fast. I began packing my duffle bag without any hesitation and soon after that they were able to get me on a "whale" which was a C-46 Navy aircraft. I waved farewell to Malta's beautiful beaches as we took off. It was really impossible to rest with the large twin-engines sending vibrations throughout the craft and I didn't feel any better knowing that the whale had a reputation of easily catching on fire and blowing up while in flight. But the flight schedule helped to take my mind off things. We stopped in North Africa, the Azores, and Iceland before getting back to Norfolk; so, the trip took a couple of days. I was a little anxious because had I not arrived on time, I would have missed the training cycle. But we made it.

Up until this time UDT frogmen were basically WWII white Navy veterans that were held in high esteem. They had a solid reputation for never having left any man behind in battle. It was a little like an elite club. And then came my friend Bernie. Bernard Waddell was the only east coast

African American Frogman recruit. He graduated a year before I arrived.

He wrote a book ("I Am Somebody: The True Story of a Black United States Navy Frogman") where he said UDT Frogmen had a proud tradition as the Navy's "noblesse" and underwent the most difficult training in the U.S. military—and perhaps the whole world. They had an attrition rate between 70 -85 percent. But as an African American, Bernie kind of paved the way for me. He said the day he reported for training, heads turned, eyeballs swiveled at him and right away they started whispering wisecracks about him.

He said there was one big and ugly redneck instructor who charged at him like a bull, saying "I WANT YOU" and then in a southern drawl whispered "you are in the wrong place—quit now because I'm going to give you loads of personal attention." He also asked Bernie if he was a sissy and would like to kiss his–you know what! Then he said the outfit didn't want him. But I knew that somehow we'd all get tested, and I had settled my mind not to take any insults personally. I expected to be harassed because I was told it was the roughest training in the military, and I knew that if I took it personally they would stay on me until I'd say I couldn't take it anymore. Honestly I don't think that I was harassed any more than the other guys in the class, though there were times when I sensed other team members personally didn't like me. I once overheard an instructor deliberately say that they already had one of them (referring to Bernie) in our outfit and that we didn't need another.

3

FORWARD DOUBLE-TIME

Dropouts and Survivors of Underwater Demolition Team 21

"I had an old dog his name was blue"
"I HAD AN OLD DOG HIS NAME WAS BLUE!"
"Blue Wanna be a UDT Too"
"BLUE WANNA BE A UDT TOO!"
"So I bought him a swim mask and four tiny fins"
"SO I BOUGHT HIM A SWIM MASK AND FOUR TINY FINS!"
"And I took him to the ocean and I threw him in"
"AND I TOOK HIM TO THE OCEAN AND I THREW HIM IN!"

"Blue came back to my surprise"
"BLUE CAME BACK TO MY SURPRISE!"

"With a shark in his mouth and a gleam in his eyes"
"WITH A SHARK IN HIS MOUTH AND A GLEAM IN HIS EYES!"

"Sound off"
"ONE... TWO!"
"Sound it off"
"THREE... FOUR"
"Bring–it–all–down"
"ONE... TWO... THREE... FOUR..."
"ONE... TWO... THREE... FOUR..."

The eighteen weeks of training were basically held at three locations: Norfolk, Virginia at Little Creek, Saint Thomas in the Virgin Islands, and Vieques Island off of Puerto Rico; the final four weeks were all about testing us in the water. Even at this time, a few of the guys were still intimidated by water and needed to face their fears.

The first week and a half at Little Creek was meant to get prior shipboard sailors back into shape. We worked out in a Physical Training (PT) uniform: boondockers, (a Navy issued boot), green utilities and helmet liners. Activities were organized around running, swimming and calisthenics to wake up sleeping muscles. You would see men who came in as skinny as a rail, and before they left, they had muscles on their bodies that they didn't even know existed. In the beginning we were politely told to ignore the high attrition rate, we were given pats-on-the-back and the standard 'go get 'em tiger' encouragement. Then we were reminded that there was not one recorded instance of any UDT man ever abandoning a swim buddy and that our minds could function as the master over a half-dead, incapacitated, totally exhausted body if we would allow it. The pressure grew.

At Little Creek we were built up slowly with a regular 10-minute run followed by a three-minute walk. They repeated this run, walk, run again drill and added more minutes every day. By the end of the first week, we weren't walking anymore, and the runs were pushed to an hour or longer. Before long this workout became a hard run in boots through sand. But I had discovered during PT that running was one of my greatest strengths. I was an exceptional runner among my classmates. In fact, I was so enthused that after the training session I and two buddies decided to register for the Boston Marathon. But again, I was officially told that "coloreds" were not allowed to compete. There were still some things we could do, and some things we couldn't. My two classmates would register without me.

But the training went on and they were on us every day to try to get us to quit. They yelled at us from nose to nose:

"YOU PUKE!
QUIT, YOU PUKE!
YOU AIN'T GONNA MAKE IT—
WE'RE GONNA GRADUATE THIS CLASS IN A TELEPHONE BOOTH!"

They wanted to see how much you could take because the last thing they ever wanted to see was someone quit mid-term on a real mission. If you messed up in training they would just say 'okay, give me a hundred push-ups' while they took a long hard look at how you responded. They noticed everything and I started to panic when one said to me 'oh, we see that your trigger finger is gone.' But right away I explained I was left-handed, which wasn't a lie because I'm ambidextrous; I bowl, play golf and do most things left-handed—except write. They could see that I wasn't making an issue about it and decided to follow suit.

I was thankful and relieved. In the end I was able to get through by slipping the nub of my index finger across the trigger guard to fire my weapons. They had never thought about it, but there were no left-handed rifles; if I were to shoot my automatic weapon left-handed all of the hot bullet casings would have been ejected towards me and would have fallen down the inside of my shirt fatigues—and this would have burned like hell.

There were about 26 obstacles on the Obstacle Course with the zig-zag line supposedly being the easiest. It had three ascending logs with gaps making it impossible to step from one to another. You had to jump from log to log while keeping your balance.

There was also The High Net, which was a fifty-feet high cargo net requiring you to climb up one side and down the other. The Belly Robber had logs placed chest-high which you had to jump into stomach-first, and weave over and under. And the Slide for Life was a wooden tower with two ropes hanging down from one side over deep, thick muddy waters. You had to climb on a rope at a thirty-degree angle and slide on your chest. All of the 26 challenges had to be done in under 15 minutes.

We did activities for about fourteen hours a day in guerilla warfare training including crawling and worming through mud to evade detection. They didn't emphasize classroom training during the first few weeks as I figured they needed to wear us out first. But later we were taught about historic Navy figures like Admiral Kauffman, the "Father of Demolition," who trained the Naval Combat Demolition Units (NCDUs) that were first on the beaches at the Normandy invasion. Others were sent to the Pacific UDTs. It was interesting, but I was looking forward to the next phase, waterborne test drills.

Swimming was obviously a large part of training and started with pool swims of a few hundred yards. You could only use two strokes—a breaststroke and a side stroke. Your hands couldn't come out of the water and the rationale behind that was if someone's looking for you from a plane, they wouldn't be able to see any splashes. They increased our swim by 200-yard increments until the final one-mile swim before they started to emphasize leg kicks. They were preparing us to use fins, which we would need later for an eight-mile swim test.

We were taught about the use of large and small Inflatable Boats (IBL and IBS). The IBS was 300 pounds, and we had to carry it on our heads while we ran. We had to take it everywhere we went and sometimes we had to carry an instructor inside. With the IBL, they would make us complete a traditional "Around the World" challenge to practice a team response in a mock amphibious crisis. Each seven-man crew had to carry this eight feet wide craft, which weighed over 400 pounds. The shorter guys got away with bearing a lighter load as their arm length couldn't match the taller ones. Sometimes they would just barely be touching the craft with the tips of their fingers. But we ran through hundreds of yards in swamps, carrying or paddling in the boat. We crossed over seawalls in the dark, stepping over barbed wire while instructors pushed us to give "every ounce" we had—and "Hell Week" hadn't even started yet.

The majority quit after the first five to six weeks. All you had to do was take your helmet off, set it down, ring a bell and '*sayonara*,'—no one would hold anything against you. You would just find yourself on a ship somewhere doing ship duty. But Hell Week was designed for one simple specific purpose: To make as many men as possible drop out of UDT training. The physical and mental demands went beyond a natural man's capacity to endure, making him rely basically on will-power. We all knew it was coming, but still it came as a shock.

They interrupted our sleep with the sound of an explosion. Then the barrack lights were flipped on and an instructor started ran-sacking the bay by overturning the two-man bunks. Everything was everywhere; trash from trash cans, sheets and ash trays were thrown towards the center of the barracks while the sounds of loud firecrackers were popping around us outside—exploding smoke grenades also made things more confusing.

For the next six days the intense training would become crazy with small rest periods. We were always on the move with racing, calisthenics, worming through mud, swimming, going over the obstacle course, lugging the IBLs wherever we went during transitions.

We all began with the IBLs on our heads—the short guys put a special number ten can on their helmets, so they'd bear their share of the weight—while instructors rode inside with a paddle to get us going. We had about eight instructors that followed us all the way through and if they said to jump off a rock you'd better jump off that rock. So, we'd run, dump the boats in the harbor and paddle out through the ferry channel. We rowed for a while, then fought currents heading for shore, landed, picked up IBLs and instructors. We must have run, limped and crawled over a distance of about twenty-one miles.

The Underwater Psychological Training (UPT) came at the end of Hell Week, and we started by taking an elevator to the top of a 112-foot water-filled tower and dropping in to practice treading through 110 feet. The instructors guided us through the hazards, and we learned to "follow the bubbles" floating up through 16 atmospheres of pressure. Only after completing our full training cycle could we then learn to master using the Pirelli oxygen rebreather, which kept any bubbles from rising in shallow water. This little piece of equipment let us do things like attach explosives to the hulls of ships without being noticed.

When we got to using the Pirelli, we could swim down to the ocean floor and do things like practice underwater Judo and track predatory fish. We got to swim with sharks. I never saw this as dangerous, but they told us if a shark came up to you, just punch it in the nose to ward it away—though we knew that at nighttime if it came up to you, it would be a different story; most likely it would chomp down on you. I remember a later incident when an officer off-duty lost his arm in a shark attack. We had to locate the fish and cut it open. When we saw the pale chewed up arm with the UDT watch still attached on it, we knew our search was over. That poor guy had bled to death.

A fun part of the training was blowing things up. We did a lot of damage on Piñero Island, where we had unlimited access to explosives for practice. After the recon of waterborne obstacles, we put demolition charges on each obstacle to blast them out of the water.

Some were hedgehog obstacles, like those on Omaha beach during D-day. Hedgehogs were made up of a series of large, interlocking steel or concrete beams, each with four or five sharp, pointed spikes. There was more to explosives than just attaching them on targets and tying them together with an explosive Prima cord trunk-line. We also had to learn how to calculate demolition charges for different types of obstacles, while also making them detonate at the same time. We became so well skilled that we could blow up any type of obstacle using plastic explosives even though all of these things were still relatively new.

With the UPT phase complete we were able to get ready for the last qualifying swim challenge; it was a free-style endurance. They let us choose to do either a breast-stroke or side-stroke with fins in the "Big Swim" from Vieques Island back to the Puerto Rico mainland at the Naval Air Station. Vieques was about eight miles from the mainland. The Atlantic Ocean surrounded the northern part of the island while the Caribbean surrounded the southern part, and the temperature difference between the two bodies of water created an undercurrent pressure. There were three different currents from Vieques to Puerto Rico and you could almost see a color change in the water showing which way the current was going. The challenge was to fight against the current pressure and keep your eyes targeted on the landmass.

By this stage, 82 of the 97 trainees that started the training cycle with me had dropped out. I was one of the remaining 15, but that number dropped to 14 when one more quit. The class included five U.S. Army Rangers—young guys right out of training from schools such as jump, ranger, or jungle warfare. They just couldn't take it. We actually had one trainee that died while free diving because he held his breath too long underwater. They said his carbon dioxide levels had increased too much.

To begin the swim from Vieques back to the Navy base

in Puerto Rico, the instructors got on paddleboards, and we waded in the water after them until we reached the starting point. They tried to keep their crafts away from us to avoid creating any ripples that could cause a disturbance—while still keeping us in view. You didn't want to get into any trouble on that swim because you could be phased out of the training on the spot. The instructors would just reach in the water and pull a trainee up on their paddleboard and that was it—I know it took me a good five hours to make the swim across, and I was a good swimmer, but I wasn't as good as the remaining majority in my class.

Several of my classmates were better than me and a few were truly exceptional. We had two guys whose feet had been so torn-up from running that they couldn't even wear any fins for the Big Swim—but they still made it ahead of all of us swimming in their bare feet.

It is impossible to describe how you feel once you've reached the mainland of Puerto Rico at the end of the swim. You are completely exhausted, hungry, and sick from accidentally gulping sea water. But then you realize that it's finally over.

At the end of the 16 weeks the remaining 14 of us established ourselves among a brotherhood of noble warriors. We were now a part of UDT-21, and it wouldn't matter how dangerous the conditions were, or how impossible the assignment seemed, a UDT Navy frogman always persevered—that was sure.

Class 17 Photo: Bill Goines, top row second from left

"I do not advertise the nature of my work, nor seek recognition for my actions. I voluntarily accept the inherent hazards of my profession, placing the welfare and security of others before my own."

—SEAL Ethos

4

THE BAY OF PIGS INVASION—ALMOST

Obviously there is a special type of bond which happens among guys who struggle through adversity together and this is how it was with our friendships on the team. They nicknamed me "Harry" because they thought I resembled the Jamaican calypso singer, Harry Belafonte—and I have to admit there was a little resemblance, largely because of our haircuts.

The social clubs on Saint Thomas island would often let me in for free because Belafonte was so popular around there. For them, he really could do no wrong. And people would tell me if I could only sing a little I might be able to get some impersonation gigs in the Caribbean on the side—but I couldn't carry a tune if it had a handle on it.

So, it seemed that everyone had a nickname, and I became seen less as a "colored" guy from Ohio when I was among my brothers. Off-base however, it was still the late 1950s—and we were in the South.

In 1958, the Virginia legislature ordered public schools to racially integrate for the first time, but the governor refused to let them do it. When his order was overturned by the state Supreme court a lot of people didn't like it and just pushed against it.

I was returning to Norfolk that April with UDT buddies from duty overseas. There were times when some of the guys who were anxious to go club-hopping would say 'C'mon, Bill, it doesn't matter what's going on in the news around here, we're goin' down to so-and-so and I'd tell them ok, you guys go on ahead—but they never wanted me to feel left out.

They would insist saying "no, you're goin' with us." So they took me to a place called Billy's Club on Shore Drive which was a very popular spot near the beach.

When we walked inside one patron sitting at the bar with a half-filled mug of beer in hand just gawked at us in disbelief. Then Billy, the owner, took notice and hurried over.

"You know *he* can't come in here!" he said, shamefully averting his head away from us to avoid making eye-contact.

But my buddies responded, "If he can't come in here we're going to turn this place out and everybody in here is going to leave."

You could see the anxiety on his face begin to surface. He became so intimidated by the united support for me that he let me in but led me to a private room where I was to remain alone.

However, in a brief moment of humanity he explained that I didn't have to pay for anything because he was going to take care of anything I wanted. I was still segregated from the rest; however, he said I could stay as long as I wanted—but to think the guys were ready to raise an uproar for me was evidence of how we were getting ahead of a slowly changing culture.

Naval Station Norfolk and the Naval Air Station Roosevelt Roads in Puerto Rico were the two most frequented locations for UDT training onthe east coast. We used a great deal of open space for our "cast and recovery" drill techniques which was one of our basic functions. It was a technique used to get men in and out of the water quickly.

An IBS would be secured to the side of a Landing Craft Personnel Ramp (LCPR) for a casting run with the IBS on the side facing away from the shore. This procedure allowed the swimmers to be kept hidden from sight and potential gunfire. We would enter the IBS in pairs or single file and watch for the controller's signal to roll over this side while the boat maintained a high speed run parallel to the beach.

During the demolition swims other UDT men would be at the stern and simultaneously toss demolition packs over the side as each pair of swimmers entered the water. After placing explosives at random markers, we all had to space out evenly to meet up at a rendezvous point. But the tricky part came on the recovery run.

When the LCPR came back to recover us, you had to raise your left arm as the boat sped towards you so that the snare man, sitting in the middle of the craft, would hook his noose over your arms to haul you back in like a fish.

It was exhilarating at first; speeding along in that LCPR felt more like flying. But it grew mundane after a while—like an amusement park ride taken too many times. Months passed and I was ready for something different. So, when they asked me to start teaching drills I thought "okay this will mix it up a little."

I left Norfolk for Puerto Rico to work as a UDT instructor in the month of February 1960. I had come full circle with the team, and I felt I had something to offer new recruits.

They all looked so young and green; or maybe I was just becoming aware of a brand new generational cycle. As the elder now I often felt I had to be both an instructor and mentor—but working as a UDT member also meant I needed to be ready for an unexpected change at any given time.

And within a year they pulled me out to work on a Top Secret mission. This was not only new to me, but it marked the beginning of new undercover assignments which would characterize a new era.

For obvious reasons we were never given a whole lot of background information about our missions. I later learned that approximately 1000 miles north of Puerto Rico in Miami Florida, other carefully selected UDT personnel had been briefed for a classified training assignment. They trained 12 designated Cuban exiles, called the Twelve Disciples, to participate in an amphibious invasion of Cuba to overthrow Fidel Castro.

President Eisenhower had planned an invasion and called it "Operation Bumpy Road." When President John F Kennedy became president in 1961, he renamed it "Operation Zapata" after the Zapata Swamp, which was located in the southern Matanzas Province of Cuba. He had barely been in office a little more than two months before the network news began running stories about the expanding problems surrounding Cuban relations.

The United States was secretly backing counter-revolutionary groups and Americans didn't want to commit troops to get involved. The president held a special press conference about it.

Kennedy actually promised that U.S. armed forces wouldn't intervene in Cuba. But on the night of April 17, 1961, five UDT trained Cuban frogmen entered the Bay of Pigs via a landing craft and got to shore so they could set up landing lights for us and others to follow.

At this time, I was on an unseen military transport ship with other frogmen in boats who were also standing by. We were waiting for a signal to enter an amphibious craft to head for the beach. We had everything we needed to make a run on Cuba being fully capable of swimming in with SCUBA gear.

The ships we used had small boats clinging to the sides and we could see Cuba over a seven-mile distance.

Our Officer in Charge said, "All right, I want you all to take off your dog tags and leave them right here, with us."

We followed the order and waited in silence. Everybody knew what they had to do and were well trained with their weapons; I had an M-16, but others had different types of guns. Our ship's insignia was painted over to make it a ghost ship; all we flew was an American flag.

Since we were in complete darkness we weren't aware of how many other transports were in the convoy but all the guys with me were excited. We were ready to go because this was what we had been training for, though we didn't know exactly where they would drop us.

Our transport kept making its way to get as close to the island as it could without drifting into a range of fire. At times, one of the guys would say he could smell odors from offshore. Then we began to notice something; all we were doing was circling in the ocean. Then the letdown; at the last minute it seemed, everything was called off.

The failure of the whole Bay of Pigs operation created pressure between the president and the National Security Council to speed up the work in making special units forces. The idea for an improved "Naval Guerrilla/Counter-Guerrilla Warfare" capability actually had already been described in a Memorandum to Admiral Arleigh Burke, the Chief of Naval Operations.

But after Kennedy did a "lessons-learned" review of the

failed run on Cuba, they decided to search for ways to strengthen guerilla and anti-guerilla teams. Then, in response to a directive from the Pentagon, officers for UDT-21 began to review our performance records to develop the world's toughest commando force. Even the president himself started making public appearances to get some new recruits.

In 1962 he spoke to West Point graduates to pitch the new special operations forces command, and it was reported in the news: People started to accept that we needed to change the military a little because Cuba now was backed by the Soviet Union, and they were threatening to down any American reconnaissance flights over their territory. Americans were also getting anxious about Communism in Vietnam—there was just a whole lot of mess going on. And at the same time race relations were getting shaken up here; that was the year James Meredith became the first African American student at the University of Mississippi, Jackie Robinson made it into the Hall of Fame and the Washington Redskins became the last pro football team to racially integrate.

So, these were unconventional times, and we needed unconventional solutions for fighting wars overseas and keeping peace in our own cities. I think it was around this time when the government really pushed for more racial integration—which was itself an unconventional tactic for the general public.

But in all of this whirlwind the plan for Navy SEALs

came through and it was perfect for those times because they were looking for highly qualified men, regardless of their racial background, to teach unconventional warfare.

In January 1962, UDT-21 was called to a muster. We were gathered behind UDT headquarters and an officer in front of the formation read off a list of names—my name might have been fourth, or fifth on that list. He read names of officers, chiefs and others—all of us were qualified for open-circuit, closed-circuit, mixed-gas diving gear and parachute jumping.

We were quietly waiting for further instructions in a classroom when I noticed muffled chatter among us—some were suspecting that another invasion force for Cuba was being put together. Once we settled and sat down however a number of starched-collared officials from Washington D.C met us to explain.

"Listen, men, we're now going to be brief. We've observed all of you for almost two years now and you have been selected from the ranks of UDT-21 as the best. We want to offer you an opportunity to be a part of a new unit called SEALs, which stands for sea, air, and land. But though you all have been hand selected for the team, you will still have to volunteer to transfer in, if you want in."

About forty of us were interviewed individually and we were told as much information that was available. I remember asking "sir what is a SEAL team and what am I expected to do?" And the officer said he couldn't talk about the missions and what we'd be doing, but I remember him saying, you'll be going to a lot of schools, and we expect you to come back here to sit down and write lesson plans for future SEAL teams.

Some men declined, choosing to remain a UDT Frogman—one young ensign even complained that it sounded too much like a suicide outfit. But I knew we would be doing more exciting things, so I accepted the offer making me the first African American Navy SEAL and plankowner (from the first class of SEALs); later, my family back home would tell me how my great, great grandfather, Daniel Hamlin, in 1864, was the first black in his unit to volunteer as a Union soldier in the Civil War.

He had left Virginia to fight for freedom in Ohio, and now here I was leaving Ohio to go back to Virginia as the first black SEAL—how things so often cycle back around!

Though SEALs became uniquely different from the other special operations forces there still is a lot of diversity among them. Even now you can't just look at a man and determine whether or not he'd make it through SEAL training. Some of us were tall, others we short; some of us were stronger than others—but we all had to prove ourselves.

The question about race was largely a non-issue; you either made the cut, or you didn't. And each of us would have over forty different training schools to attend during our time of service with specialists in the Army, Navy, Air Force and Marines teaching us.

Bill as Frogman: Underwater Training

The Navy established SEAL Team ONE at the Naval Amphibious Base (NAB) Coronado, California and SEAL Team TWO at NAB Little Creek, Norfolk, Virginia.

All of the men were taken from the ranks of UDT-11 & -12 on the west coast and UDT-21 on the east coast. Basic UDT replacement training remained the same however, the name was changed to Basic Underwater Demolition/SEAL

(BUD/S) in 1972 to create a type of standard for both frogmen and SEALs.

While UDT would continue to specialize in underwater demolition, surveying beaches, and water maneuvers; SEALs would add land-combat skills including guerrilla/counterinsurgency operations specializing in tactics out at sea, air and on land. Additional tasks were to surveil, capture or kill high priority targets and gather intelligence behind enemy lines.

"My loyalty to Country and Team is beyond reproach. I humbly serve as a guardian to my fellow Americans, always ready to defend those who are unable to defend themselves."

—SEAL Ethos

5

NOTHING COMES BETWEEN US

On paper the plan sounded all right. And we all pretty much knew each other well as UDT operators. But now there were questions about whether or not we could come together as a solid unit with new dynamics brought on by SEAL Team protocols. We needed a type of "real world" test.

Our bond of loyalty to each other underwent a test, but it wasn't on a battlefield or in a water drill; it was a test in the civilian sector, and again, I found myself at the center of it all. The entire team was scheduled to visit the Army Base Fort Bragg in North Carolina for unconventional warfare training; Bragg was the home of Army Special Forces.

We dressed in green Army fatigues with spit-shined jump boots to be inconspicuous, and we were traveling there, from Virginia, in a government bus. The convoy stopped to get breakfast at a small honkey-tonk truck-stop restaurant in North Carolina, so we got off and made our way inside nearly filling the seating capacity. The twenty or so of us broke up to sit at tables of four.

I remember a buddy, James Watson, sitting at my table: He wrote about our experience that day in a book describing how some time had passed before we noticed that all the other guys were getting their food, and we hadn't even had our orders taken yet. A waitress went by and he stopped her:

"I'm sorry ma'am, but could we please have some service?"

"Well, can I take y'alls order?" she said pretending to be hospitable in southern drawl. Then, turning to me her voice changed, and she said sternly, "But you gotta go in the back. No *coloreds* are allowed in here."

She then turned to my buddy, raised a penciled eyebrow and said "that I could go in the back and pick up a sandwich" or something like that. In an even tone she continued addressing everyone else saying "I'm sorry, but you're in North Carolina now and I won't serve this table as long as *he* is here!"

Some of the guys just sat shocked with their mouths gaping wide open. By this time, we all were so close with one another that this whole segregation thing caught us off-guard. So, at that moment one SEAL stood up and addressed the whole team saying, "Hey guys! This place won't serve a teammate!They're refusing to serve one of us."

The rest of the Team could see what the problem was and remained silent. But then, without a word, in silent protest, there was a show of loyalty in true SEAL team spirit.

As if on cue they dropped their forks and knives, stood up and we all walked out the door one-by-one ignoring complaints from the staff about their orders being almost done.

The staff gawked in disbelief. We got back into our bus and got about five minutes down the road before the state police stopped us—they made us stop because the guys hadn't paid for their food; so two of our officers got out and talked to them.

I'm not too sure what they said, but it must have been something like "you don't mess with government people." Despite our hunger, we proceeded to Fort Bragg in silent reflection without any further problems—and I got a few pats on my back.

We appeared to have passed that test; now we just had to be sure to pass all the tests at the Center for Unconventional and Psychological Warfare.

The Green Berets was one of their most notable groups so there was a whole lot of training that went on at that base. When we read the description of our required classes it looked like a college freshman's catalog of fall prerequisites—but I liked the diversity.

There was jungle warfare, kitchen-table demolitions, judo training, language school, foreign weapons, survival school, and others. Some classes like lock-picking were optional, but most were mandatory and would take years to finish at Bragg and other bases.

After you got certified in a certain skill however, you became available for special duty assignments before returning to resume classes.

For the time being we started out with a two-week class in demolitions, unconventional warfare, and firing range training. Most people don't realize that common things they have in their own house could be made into bombs.

We were taught how to go into a kitchen and blow up the place by just using common items found there—like the light bulbs, for example. We also mastered how to mix certain elements to create explosives that we would use extensively in Vietnam.

We were given training in hand-to-hand combat techniques instructing how to kill an enemy soldier and take his gun by launching a charge of broken glass with match heads, which were also handy when it came to making firearms from pieces of pipe and homemade explosives.

We got familiar with the M3 grease gun, the Thompson Submachine gun, the French MAT-49, the British Sten Mark II, the German Schmeisser and the Karl Gustav M/45 submachine gun, commonly known as the "Swedish K."

Eventually, I became a sharpshooter, despite my partially amputated finger, and after the required hours of hands-on instruction, we were split up into smaller groups to travel to different training sites around the country.

I was sent west to Stead Air Force Base (AFB) in Reno, Nevada where we learned Judo and Escape and Evasion techniques. The class was established to help Navy and Air Force pilots learn how to avoid being captured and survive in the jungle. They were also big on applying the Uniform Code of Military Justice (UCMJ).

When I arrived on base with two other SEALs, the base commander secretly pulled us aside and told us we were going to be used in a confidential exercise to see if his officers knew how to apply the UCMJ in a mock POW exercise.

"Listen," he said, "you boys are from the SEALs aren't you?"

"Yes sir."

"Welcome to Stead. We want to use you three in a short little demonstration for our officers."

Though the tone of his voice was easygoing, the insignia of the eagle on his pressed blue uniform conveyed a different tone, so we knew better than to decline his wishes.

"I want you boys to stage a fight amongst yourselves—it doesn't have to go on too long, only long enough for someone to come and break it up. We're just doing a review in codes of conduct for POWs, and I need to know if we're all learning anything."

The three of us talked it over and decided we would fight over a cigarette. They were to jump me. So, during an assembly, we positioned ourselves so that everyone could see us arguing and shouting at each other.

We ramped up the heat. But then something unexpected happened. One of the guys drew back his fist to throw a fake punch, but it actually landed hard along the side of my head, triggering me to respond in a fury. It made me so mad that it turned out to be a real fight. The two guys jumped me and we were going fist to fist.

When the SEAL Officer in Charge (OIC) broke it up, he just couldn't believe what he had seen. We were escorted to the base commander.

"I should have knocked y'all's heads off!" he said. Thankfully the base commander interrupted:

"No, your boys did alright. It was all a setup. I chose the three of them to act out this demonstration for us. Don't come down on them. They did a great job!"

Still pissed at us: "Why didn't y'all tell me this?"

"We wanted to, sir," I said, looking up at him, "but the base commander said no one was supposed to know."

He then composed himself a little and said in a calmer tone that he just couldn't believe his eyes when he saw two SEALs fighting each other!

A code of honor had been drummed into us from the beginning that there were to be no disputes among SEALs and that we were expected to "have each other's backs" at all times—like back at that truck stop in North Carolina.

Bill Goines in civilian clothing, seen with SEAL TWO teammate Chief Petty Officer Jim Tipton

Sometimes we might have seen ourselves as misfits, but there were no minorities, per se, among us and this was thanks to the training and our reciprocal support system.

"I will never quit. I persevere and thrive on adversity. My Nation expects me to be physically harder and mentally stronger than my enemies. If I get knocked down, I will get back up, every time."

—SEAL Ethos

6

THE FIRST TOUR IN 'NAM

I lived by my own "failure-is-no-option" self-pledge and people saw it. This consequently helped me to achieve a measure of respect that many civilian black males had been striving for at that time. I was able to maximize my opportunities by impressing upon my commander that I was willing for any assignment, and I even went out of my way to volunteer for a special mission.

The government had called the plan "Operation Strategic Hamlet" which started in March 1962. We had been called to work with the South Vietnamese to protect their people in the farming areas from being influenced by the Communist backed Viet Cong (VC) without using any military action. But the plan began to fall apart as more VC began moving into the countryside. They had their ways of quiet, stealthy infiltration to win the hearts of the people. As a result, Kennedy increased military assistance to strengthen a counterinsurgency plan and make the Army of The Republic of Viet Nam (ARVN) stronger. The ARVN needed advisors and teachers, and I was ready to take on the responsibility of either role. But I and the guys who went with me understood that we wouldn't have immunity from any sniper bullets. Anything could happen in the field. Even so, we packed up and flew to Saigon on a commercial airliner.

Excited again, we were going over there to teach hand-to-hand combat, weaponry, small boat tactics—anything that we knew, though we, ourselves, were still in our infancy. We hadn't yet been to a whole lot of schools ourselves, but when we got to Vietnam we rented a 'safe house' in the middle of the city where we became like a school. We did a lot of training there with interpreters who could speak Chinese, Vietnamese, and Montagnard—the language of the tribal people. We trained from Monday to Saturday.

Bill Goines at left with SEAL Team TWO platoon mates displaying "pets" found in their Mekong Delta operating region in South Vietnam

Because our SEAL unit had not yet received any ammunition for M-16 training, U.S. Army Special Forces advisors stationed 20 minutes away worked with locals emphasizing infantry field training. They were expected to observe, draw conclusions, give counsel and teach; and they had to train with live ammunition because sometimes the exercises reverted to a live gunfight with VC guerillas nearby.

They showed them how to use Claymore anti-personnel mines, which they later used against night-traveling bands of guerillas. With cloth, pipe cleaner, lubricant and que-tips; they learned to systematically clean M-16 rifles. They had to remove the magazines, disassemble them and check for any traces of sandy soil. But we trained them rigorously in hand-to-hand combat maneuvers which were based upon Judo leveraging techniques. We tried to make their training as practical as possible for facing their enemy on a jungle battlefield. The VC used traditional hand combat weapons like a Japanese type 30 bayonet, spears and blades; when they ambushed you they often tried to stab you just under the chin. To defend yourself from a frontal right-handed attempt at a stab under the chin or near the neck, we instructed them to pivot to the left and strike downward on the assailant's arm, take hold of his wrist with the left hand and give a quick elbow jab to the face. After being stunned by the jab, they could encircle his neck with their left arm, bring him to a half-choke hold and drop him to the floor with a "Maki-Komi" hard body fall on top of that arm. In most cases, this would break his arm.

To treat jungle battle wounds, we had to improvise a little with available field resources. Gunshot wounds to the head required padded direct pressure to control the bleeding using bulky dressing. From the neck to the lower rib cage, a bullet round could create a sucking chest wound so we told them to place a hand over the injury to stop the suction and put a thin sheet of plastic tape over it to block air intake.

Gunshot wounds to the stomach always required a lot of bulky dressing that you couldn't remove. But for gunshot wounds to the arm, they had to apply direct pressure, bulky dressing and if necessary a tourniquet. We weren't supposed to remove any protruding punji stakes from wounds because those we had to cushion with gauzes and padding until they could be removed at a medical facility.

We tried to cover every possible treatment for expected and unexpected injuries until I started coming down with something and needed my own treatment. It was an unknown disease. My hand was rotting away—actually rotting away. It was scary because I was losing complete control of my hand. They transported me to Station Hospital Saigon, which had been converted from a former hotel, where I was relieved to hear the doctor explain that my case of "jungle rot" was treatable.

"All right, let's see what you got?" he said, wheeling over to me on a stool. He took hold of the bend in my elbow to flip my hand from side to side, studying it.

"Yeah, we've seen this before but it's a good thing you're here now because in some of these cases we've had to amputate—but we can get you back in the jungle in about two weeks—give the medication a chance to kill all of that mycobacteria and keep your hands dry."

Our tours of duty were different from the Army or Marines; we weren't ordered to fight in Vietnam, but rather we were offered a cycle of six-month voluntary deployments, which we could have declined without any consequences. Under extreme circumstances we might be asked to remain seven or eight months. When the final weeks of my first tour were over I reflected on what I had learned about South Vietnamese Culture and their urgent need for training in modern warfare. I knew a massive buildup of U.S. infantry loomed on the horizon because the VC were coming up with new methods of making inroads into the southern region. I thought about returning, but there would be several new SEAL training courses to master first. A relatively new parachuting training method called High Altitude Low Opening (HALO) jumping was waiting for me at Ft. Bragg. But before training, I would have to stop at Patuxent River Naval Air Station in Maryland to help screen more possible UDT-SEAL recruits.

"*We expect to lead and be led. In the absence of orders I will take charge, lead my teammates and accomplish the mission. I lead by example in all situations.*"

—SEAL Ethos

7

JUMPMAN TROPHY

The Patuxent River Naval Air Station was about 65 miles southeast of Washington DC and they basically did research and tested aircraft.

There were about ten men on base who were interested in becoming either a SEAL or UDT frogman—and two were African American. All ten were good recruits but our only job there was to lay out training expectations. One of them asked:

"How good of a swimmer do I need to be to get in the Navy SEAL program?"

"Well, you'll have to pass the 500-yard swim test in under twelve minutes and thirty seconds, and you need to be able to use different strokes."

"I was ranked among the top ten swimmers on my high

school swim team, do the instructors consider the high school records?"

"Having that kind of background can give you a little advantage but in the end you've still got to pass the tests and Hell week. These are not just physical tests—you've got to be mentally strong too. So don't let your past accomplishments give you a false sense of security because the tests are tough."

"Yes, sir."

My teammate and I very soberly answered questions about training, risks on waterborne missions, Vietnam and the importance of being adaptable. We knew these men were at a crossroad in their lives and we were hopeful for them.

The three-day screening session did me a lot of good because it allowed me to readjust from the pace of life in Vietnam back to the regimented rhythm of a training school.

It was a type of a 'cool down' lap before gearing up for these new high-altitude jumps—and I felt good about returning to Bragg. It was like a home away from home.

Like superheroes we were free falling in the sky reaching a terminal velocity faster than 160 miles per hour. The earth always looked like quilted patchwork on our descent before the sudden jerk on our canopy lowered us like a huge airbrake.

In HALO jumping we opened our parachutes at a predetermined altitude, assembled in the air, navigated under a canopy, and landed together as a tactical unit. This was the preferred way to infiltrate whenever the skies were safe enough.

SEALs were supposed to maneuver in the air and land together at a predetermined drop zone (DZ) tracking through the air with our legs straightened and arms tucked close to our bodies. The guys generally liked the idea of HALO jumping because it was stealthy.

Since we used only a little forward airspeed no one could detect us on radar and our chutes were only open for a short period of time, so the enemy hardly had a chance to see us.

We, in SEAL TEAM 2 were most likely the first military unit to be trained for HALO jumping and I found myself being the first of the first.

I was the top 'jump' man in my HALO class, and I just couldn't wait to go back up and do another jump. Our instructors of the 82nd Airborne unit created a "Jumpman" award trophy and gave it to me for distinguished excellence —but we were all just having fun because it was such an exhilarating experience.

Bill Goines was in the first SEAL Team TWO class to complete the U.S. Army's Military Free Fall (MFF) training at Fort Bragg, North Carolina. Here he is seen receiving the award as the class top graduate

Before we got to jump out of any aircraft the instructor on base was always telling us to keep our feet together, knees bent and to jump straight away from the platform. And we had to try to land on all contact points: the balls of our feet, our calves, our thighs, and our butts.

We practiced this jump roll and recovery training from an elevated platform which had a simulated aircraft door frame.

We had to adjust to temperature extremes. When we jumped at a high altitude it was bitter cold, but as we were falling the atmosphere got warmer every thousand feet or so.

It could be freezing at high altitude but 90 degrees on the ground, so the jumping technique was to unzip and peel off layers as we were falling because there was always the slim possibility that we could die from heat exhaustion before we hit the ground.

We experimented with different planes to see which was the best to carry a SEAL platoon, or squad–and they thought my stability in the air was flawless. From my diving position to the free-falling stage I was able to control my glides without any flat spins or tumbling.

We were to continue testing our HALO capabilities with six aircraft: the L-20, C1 Alpha, the SP Neptune, UH-34 and UH-46 helicopters, and an A3 Skywarrior which was a jet-powered carrier-capable strategic bomber.

The L-20 was a good craft that later went through a make-over for search and rescue missions. The C-1A

"Trader" had been around since the 1950s assigned to the Carrier On-board Delivery (COD) mission, but they were originally meant to be land-based.

They were the last piston-engine aircraft to operate on the carriers and supported our parachuting operations, but you had the sense that since the SEALs were a type of new team, they probably should have designed new aircraft for us.

Despite the different planes, our jump protocol was consistent. We had to know the psychological effects of oxygen use and the operation of oxygen equipment. HYPOXIA was something that some of us would experience first-hand.

The most common symptoms were tunnel vision, color blindness, dizziness, headaches, numbness and fainting. Back then you had to use oxygen when you were higher than 20,000 feet.

I remember we had a guy who had passed out with his oxygen mask still on; he was just sitting in the door of the airplane. When they realized he was out they had to quickly yank him back in before he fell outside to his death.

Eventually there were some standard operating procedures which came out of all of this. One was called the "PRICE" check; each letter of the acronym represented a specific item of oxygen equipment:

- **P—*Pressure.*** They would check for full pressure on the system in use.

- **R—*Regulator.*** They would check everything on the regulator in use looking for dents, cracks, broken gauges and movement of dials.
- **I—*Indicator.*** They would check to make sure the flow indicator showed that gas was flowing from the storage system.
- **C—*Connections.*** They would check all hose connections
- **E—*Emergency Equipment.*** They would do a complete price check on any emergency oxygen equipment and bailout system.

The pilots of the 82nd Airborne were told to take us no higher than 20,000 feet, but in a Navy A3 we coaxed the pilots to climb higher. We didn't know any better—jumping out of an airplane at 300 miles per hour was *definitely* not normal, but three hundred miles an hour at 30,000 feet was a thrill.

Normally you jump out of a plane going about 100 miles per hour, but it was also refreshing to soar at those speeds because the heat and humidity of those North Carolina skies in August were something else.

No one had heard about helicopter jumps before the Vietnam War, the UH-34 and UH-36 gave us a 360-degree panoramic view of the landscapes which gave us a visual advantage for jungle warfare. By this time of training, we knew all the jump commands.

HALO training was one of my favorite sessions and I

appreciated how the 82nd Airborne division went beyond the call of duty and looked out for us since our Navy uniforms gave us such high visibility on that sometimes unfriendly Army base.

"*I am forged by adversity.*"
—SEAL Ethos

8

LIVING HIS DREAM IN SEALs

On a Wednesday morning in late August there was a different vibe on the base. They put one of their units on standby alert to assist in an expected civil upheaval at the nation's capital. News reports were showing thousands of people going to D.C in a civil rights protest to demand changes for blacks. Martin Luther King's "March on Washington" was underway and base Army units were to be ready. It had a feel for being something historic. But as King was talking about his dream that blacks wouldn't be judged by the color of their skin, but by their character, I felt that I was beginning to fulfill part of that dream in the SEALs.

Three months after the end of HALO training I was sitting on my bunk at Little Creek reviewing my schedule for the next training session. Amid the usual joking and prodding among the guys on base someone came sprinting through the sleeping quarters gripping a little pocket transistor radio in his hand: "Dy'a hear any of this? They shot him—they actually shot the president!"

One of the guys was fed up with all the joking, "man, if this is another stupid joke the OIC is gonna have you shot, and I'm volunteering for the firing squad."

"No! Listen, it's from ABC" he said, pushing his hand with the radio towards our faces.

We all got in a huddle around him. You could tell something important was going on at the station because some of the newsmen sounded choked up and they were all stammering like they were out of breath. They had a reporter from Dallas transmitting short bits of information from a hospital and it appeared that the Texas governor had been shot too. We were still hoping for the best when they quoted what Mrs. Kennedy's secret service agent said—that the president was "dead." But at that instant it was still something we wouldn't believe. We all could identify with JFK because he was the man who brought us together. But then, when reality hit, and a newsman confirmed the report of his death, it was so heartbreaking it made you want to do something. And we knew we'd be involved in something if they found out who was behind this; but, of course, everything was blamed on Oswald.

The president had visited Little Creek only a few months before this happened to review members of SEAL Team Two. I think he was proud of the plan to beef up special forces. He was supposed to talk about it in a campaign speech on the day of his assassination. But, of course, he would never make the meeting.

President Kennedy greets SEALs, boards USS Northampton, Navy Air Station Norfolk

On the eve of Thanksgiving some people were guessing that President Lydon B. Johnson might cut back on some of Kennedy's plans for national defense and a civil rights bill. No one really knew what to expect. But when the new president said in his speech that we would keep our commitments from "South Vietnam to West Berlin" we knew the SEALs were safe. By the end of 1963 there were already around 16,000 U.S. advisors in Vietnam.

Now there was new talk about sending combat-ready ground troops.

I had to complete twelve-month sessions of language and gunnery school before my second tour in Vietnam. This time they made me a Point-Man for my squad. I would have to lead a patrol through terrain and spot enemy targets; it was among the most dangerous positions for enemy engagement, though I would have the widest field of vision which was an advantage.

"*The ability to control my emotions and my actions, regardless of circumstance, sets me apart from others.*"

—SEAL Ethos

9

SHOOTING FROM THE HIP–SECOND TOUR

The undergrowth of terrain in South Vietnam made it easier for snipers to hide and set traps. And the Viet Cong high command was working overtime to get weapons to the South using the waterways that connected with the Mekong Delta. To make things worse, there were over a thousand miles of waterways.

The U.S. Army had already started a "seek-find-and-destroy" operation to stop VC guerillas who dressed in black pajama-like outfits to make you think they were fishermen. They used traditional man-made "junk" boats to smuggle supplies, and our Navy was using the Patrol Boat Riverine (PBRs) to police the waterways.

On January 1, two PBRs patrolling the river near a creek made contact with a junk which was quickly trying to pull out. When one PBR turned towards it, the other moved in closer to block it. Then about five gunmen jumped out and opened fire, so the first PBR just raked it with return fire.

Three VC were shot and killed while another fell overboard and was believed dead, and another was taken prisoner. When sailors of the second PBR pulled alongside the junk to inspect it they found a large amount of Communist Type-53 machine guns, drums of ammunition, anti-tank rockets, rounds of rifle ammunition and about 500 grenades.

This type of scene became common near some of the waterways and although it was a good thing to confiscate all of that ammunition, success for SEALs was more about capturing people.

You just don't go in and try to shoot people because you don't get any information like that—all you get is captured weapons which really isn't a whole lot. But, of course, sparing the life of the enemy is not always realistic.

We got intelligence reports indicating that a group of VC was occupying a village hut on a small island nearby. My squad of seven men was tasked to make a capture; so we strategized, geared up and got underway in our SEAL Team Attack Boat (STAB). We felt a sense of self-restraint once we were inserted on the shore.

The reeds along the island's edge were tall, thick and coarse. Then we came upon powdery dirt. I kept myself in a tight crouched position making mental notes of anything that might be unusual in the landscape.

Tripwire was usually strung across the trails. We were fully aware of how booby traps triggered by the wire could alert the enemy and blow the whole operation—or get us all killed! Dangerous, but exciting.

When we found the bamboo hut I stopped while the men watched for my signal. I gave them an "okay" sign and led them inside tightly gripping my shotgun at waist level ready to spray if need be.

We sneaked in and found four men sleeping on cots. It was tense and things could have easily gone wrong if we had been spotted, but we knew we had our STAB boats waiting along the shore for a quick exit. Then one man stirred and woke up. He saw us and looked as if he had seen a ghost. When he tried to jump up one of my guys just grabbed and strong-armed him into a hold.

Then the others awoke. We just wrestled, man-handled and body-slammed them into submission. We lined them up into a single file and connected all of them by tying a bowline knot around their necks which controlled their every movement.

They could only move forward. But within seconds of leaving the hut, rapid rifle fire came from everywhere. You could hear rounds whizzing by like loud insects. Though I was a sharpshooter we carried our rifles in a fire-ready position at waist level.

Since the enemy could jump out of a bush five feet away from us, we didn't have time to raise our weapons to eye-level and peer through the gunsight. We shot from the hip.

I immediately spotted a target, quickly returned fire and killed an assailant—I watched him fall hard. We knew we were in an ambush and had to move out quickly, but we then noticed that one of the prisoners had hand grenades tied to his legs. We must have overlooked them during our rushed search because we were trying to get out so fast.

Of course we had to be more careful handling that man while still taking on enemy fire, but we nonetheless had to get out immediately; so I radioed for a capability called "Puff the Magic Dragon" which was a USAF C130 that had 50 caliber weapons trained on our location.

They knew where we were because we had reflected tabs on our hats. Flying somewhere between 24 and 25 thousand feet, they shot a pattern of rounds around us creating a barrier until we got out to the boat and got away. The mission was completed, and afterwards they gave me a Combat V award for courage under fire.

COMMANDER
IV CORPS AND IV CORPS TACTICAL ZONE

Republic of Viet-Nam
Armed Forces
IV Corps
IV Corps Tactical Zone
Chief of Staff
General Adjutant Office

- Reference Memorandum #10-B dated 15 August 1950 to create the "Cross of Gallantry".
- Reference decree #74-B dated 15 August 1950 and the following letters to fix the procedure to award the "Cross of Gallantry".
- Reference Memorandum #1472/TTL/VP/PCP/3 dated 21 May 1965 to fix the authority to award the "Cross of Gallantry".
- Reference Memorandum #757/TTM/VP/PCP/3 dated 16 March 1966 to fix the regularity to award the medal to the Foreigner

*GOINES, WILLIAM J. - SK2 - 282 21 31 - U.S. NAVY

Petty Officer GOINES is a brave military man with much experience in the Seal Team missions. He participated in operations at IV Corps Tactical Zone. Particularly significant were his actions on 14 June 1967 in an operation which was attacked by the enemy at WS.822.268. While his friends received fire by Viet Cong he bravely suppressed and caused severe damage to the enemy. The result of this action was one Viet Cong killed, two Viet Cong killed which were carried away and three Viet Cong wounded. One Russian rifle and one Carbine M1 were captured. Three Viet Cong bunkers were destroyed and one explosion was caused. One of the Viet Cong killed was a platoon leader with many important documents.

CITATION AT REGIMENT LEVEL WITH AWARD OF
CROSS OF GALLANTRY WITH BRONZE STAR

APO. 34.02 dated 12 July 1964

Major General NGUYEN VAN MANH
Commander of IV Corps and IV Tactical Zone

CERTIFIED TO BE A TRUE TRANSLATION:

B. L. LEVIN, LCDR, USN
Assistant FOURTH Riverine Area Advisor

Bill Goines is awarded the Cross of Gallantry

There was another incident where we were setting up an ambush formation and we started hearing voices. I saw one male and three females gathering some kind of fruit, so we stopped them on the spot and had our interpreter tell them that we needed the man to lead us to where we suspected VC might be located—we knew they were in the vicinity. He led us to a hidden house that intelligence had identified as a VC safe haven. Somehow an occupant from inside must have been alerted because he took off running and we had to shoot him down before he could get away. Our prisoner guide then, still at gunpoint, led us to the capture of other VC in the area.

With all of the captures we were doing, lessons about the right type of weapons were still important. There was one incident where my buddy and I were carrying shotguns as point-men and the main group was in the village trying to find the enemy. Then we spotted VC walking towards the tree line. When they spotted us they started firing but there was nothing we could do with a shotgun. We could not return fire. I told my buddy that he'd better get his head down so we both got down as deep as we could in that rice patty as bullets were popping all around us. Luckily someone from the squad came up to see what was happening and we were able to point in the direction of the enemy, so they returned fire. But I decided then to never use a shotgun again. A shotgun was good when everything was close—if you come around a corner and you've got two or three guys there you could blast them away. But when you're

200 yards away they can just take pot shots at you. The diversity of terrain in Vietnam had you thinking all of the time about the most appropriate weapon for the next mission.

Another thing that started to make captures difficult was their defensive tunnel system. Sometimes an entire village was hidden underground with rooms made to be hospitals, kitchens and even theaters. Hundreds of feet below the ground they kept ammunition and ran a system of pop-up trap doors on the jungle floor. They even had suicidal attack shifts where they would attach a rope to a young soldier, put him above ground and make him shoot against U.S. troops until someone from our side finally took him out. But then they would drag his body down through the trap door and send someone else up to replace him. It made them seem invincible—like they had an unbreakable defense position. But the Army started using personnel they called 'tunnel rats' to search out these guys.

"*I am never out of the fight.*"

—SEAL Ethos

10

BUGS, CRITTERS AND PANTYHOSE

We knew that the amphibious nature of SEAL duty obviously meant that a good portion of our missions would require some type of waterborne activities. And we got used to it. But, I don't think anyone really got comfortable with the pests in the water which could just drain your energy—nagging parasites.

The leeches in Vietnam were huge and slimy and your skin was a magnet to them. Somehow they got under shirts, into pants and could even survive on land. The canals in our area contained a whole lot of leeches and they would ping on you until they sucked out a whole lot of blood.

I came up with an idea that improved body protection for squad water patrols. When I noticed one of the men complaining about leeches I said I would write to my wife and ask her to send some panty hose.

At first I had to reassure her that there was no hanky-panky going on with local women because some of her friends suspected that the term "leech" was only a code name for local gals. They would say "yeah, I'll bet he needs them for leeches alright, is that what they're calling them these days?"

But I got her to send some extra-large sizes because we had some huge guys on the squad. We would stick our feet in and stretch the hose all the way up our bodies, then spray it with insect repellent—and in the end, that's what kept the leeches off of us.

The nylon-based fibers in the panty hoses were perfect to retain insect repellent even in water. After that I wrote about the success of the new adaptation in a report and then the idea circulated to other squads. Eventually, my commander praised me for it. A few years after that some of the men started wearing blue jeans on missions for much of the same reason.

I still chuckle a little when I think about having to fight off bugs and critters during our combat missions. On one mission a buddy and I were getting ready for a night ambush, so we had to squat down and dig in the dirt a little. Then he started doing something SEALs aren't supposed to do—he started to twitch and squirm:

"Hey Bill, do you feel something? Something is biting

the hell out of me!" He started slapping at his neckline more frantically.

"Listen, you'll blow this whole operation if you don't stop." Then I started feeling the intense pinch bites all over.

Neither of us could take it anymore. We were standing up to pat and scratch our exposed skin when we realized we had squatted right in the middle of a red ant nest—and they stung.

They were so aggressive we stopped thinking about the ambush and could have probably been sniped by the enemy with all the movements we were making.

The snakes were deadly. In Vietnam you had Asian cobras, king cobras, coral snakes, kraits and different vipers. There were around 37 types of poisonous snakes. The Army called one of them "two-step" because the word was you could only walk two steps after being bitten before you dropped dead.

At a certain time, the Army was saying that once their units occupied ground, their number one enemy was often snakes and at one point snake bites had killed more infantrymen than combat wounds.

"I serve with honor on and off the battlefield."

—SEAL Ethos

11

SOCIAL PROGRESS BACK HOME

Back in Norfolk my wife continued sending news clips in my care packages about local military items of interest. In this way I learned that although race relations close to the bases seemed to still be under strain, some progress was being made.

Because of segregation blacks were often left with no other choice than to patronize shady businesses.

And it became a problem for military bases overseas too. There was a story about the state of Montana having only one restaurant opened to blacks from a nearby air base, but that restaurant was also a house of ill repute.

Military units, like SEALs, might have been desegregated but Norfolk, near our home base in Little-Creek, was just starting to get there.

By now the Johnson administration started using the

Civil Rights Acts to pressure base commanders to protect blacks from local discrimination—and some commanders had a problem with this. Officers were simply refusing to accept the idea that improving off-base relations was important to their base mission.

There was a Department of Defense (DOD) committee of civilians saying that racial discrimination in the military and nearby communities should be eliminated and also that base commanders should use sanctions against off-base businesses that discriminated against black servicemen. As a result, you could begin to see a gradual change.

I had heard a story about the commanding officer at Navy Station Norfolk putting out a notice after talking to the Norfolk city council.

I wasn't around then because I was deployed. He directed his dispersing office to pay military personnel only in two-dollar bills and he asked them to spend the money in the community when they went on liberty.

He later went to the city council and suggested that they check with the local bars and restaurants to see how many two-dollar bills had been collected in circulation. The amount of two-dollar bills was beyond their imagination, though I'm not sure what the total was.

Then he said to them if his colored staff couldn't go everywhere the whites went, he would restrict everyone to the base to use only military clubs—and that changed things. The money made a big difference because economically someone would have gone broke.

When I got back to Norfolk after my six-month tour I wasn't harassed by any of the anti-war protestors waiting at the airport like some of the soldiers or Marines experienced. We didn't come home to any crowds, but to quiet on the base.

There was a whole lot of loud talk however about a Supreme Court case in Virginia allowing a marriage between a black woman and a white man for the first time. Both of them had served jail time but won an appeal against the state. The Loving v. Virginia Case made history with a unanimous Supreme Court decision.

This demonstrated that some social progress was being made, but regardless of all of the new gains for civil rights it still never occurred to me that I was the first African American Navy SEAL. I just never really thought about it. I had a buddy however who stood out a little more as the first African American Master Navy diver.

And he caught hell! I had never had anyone jump in my face and call me the "N" word—I don't know what I would have done if they did—but he had to train with men who did things like that and even threatened to drown him.

That was Carl Brashear, and Twentieth Century Fox did a movie about him called "Men of Honor" with Robert De Niro. Carl and I had similar backgrounds.

Also, my wife and his girlfriend knew each other from our church. I would work out with him at the Norfolk base shortly after he lost his leg in that tragic accident on the ship.

He was a tough guy. We would run laps around the track together. However during those times prosthetic limbs were not what they are today, and I would watch him take that limb off after our run and blood would just be dripping from it.

"Carl," I would say, "you oughta just go to sick bay for that–can't they fix you up?"

"Yea, but after they fix me up, they'll write me up and I don't want anything on record to slow things down—you know what I mean?

I know they're waiting for an excuse to discharge me. But I'm going to make Master Diver whatever it takes. Anyway, after I soak this stump (amputated leg) in hot water and salt, the bleeding stops."

And there we were. It was good to know Carl and I sometimes had thoughts about the similarities and differences in our lives.

We were two black servicemen striving to advance. I, with a partial missing finger, was still able to fire a weapon but Carl, with an amputated leg, was trying to prove he could still be mobile while bearing the weight of nearly 300 pounds of diving gear.

In addition, he had to pas all of their physical tests to recertify. It reminded me that no matter how hard personal trials became, you didn't have to look too far to find someone else striving through something worse.

Carl never really complained, and he ended up being not only the first African American Navy Master Diver but the first amputee diver to be recertified. Thanks to him it's now possible for anyone who has been injured on active duty to be able to stay in if they can pass the physical tests.

My wife had been regularly attending a Memorial Baptist church during my assignments and when I got back it was refreshing to go together. This church dated back before the Civil War, and they were big on preaching the gospel of salvation through Jesus Christ and advancing social development.

They had their work cut out for them because by this time news stories about the war were always on T.V. and anti-war protests were growing along with race riots.

I remember one member there who had been a Tuskegee Airman from World War II—and I really credit *them* for breaking the color barriers because they had guys facing court marshals for entering a white officers' club when they had none of their own.

I got back during the month of November but, during the previous October, the first national anti-war demonstration was held in Washington. Hundreds of protestors were arrested and dragged away.

And just a month before that they had the "summer of love" events hosting a lot of free outside peace concerts with an angry anti-war theme mixed in. I had left jungle warfare to come back to all of this civilian warfare set in motion.

But I couldn't let any of these things phase me. The SEALs were good to me. I was enjoying what I was doing so much that I was always thinking about the next training phase; so I reported to Fort Lejeune to get my Field Medical Training out of the way before doing my third tour in Vietnam.

"*I persevere and thrive on adversity.*"

—SEAL Ethos

12

A NEW NETWORK, A NEWER STRATEGY

Field medical training at Lejeune was short, sweet, and action-packed. It was actually put together during World War II to get non-medical personnel combat ready for medic work.

Then they went through their phases of base closures and reactivations before and after the Korean War, but in '67 they were getting their air facility ready to be turned into the first helicopter Marine Corps Air Station.

In training they demonstrated that the best medicine during a firefight was clearly maintaining fire superiority. But they also did a great job teaching updated basic life support and casualty care procedures.

It became obvious to me that the one thing we needed to do for a wounded casualty was to simply stop the guy from bleeding to death which was a growing problem on the battlefield. Tourniquets now were the things that could save the day, even though the reality of beating an enemy that was nearly invisible in combat was becoming a complex problem too.

It was around this time when a couple of SEALs were thinking about officially improving a top-secret counterterrorism program for South Vietnam which would change the whole dynamic of stealth operations at the local level.

The Delta region, where I had led several missions as a point man, was always a hot spot for terrorism, so they came up with a pilot program they called the Delta Reconnaissance Unit which later became the Provisional Reconnaissance Unit Program (PRU).

Selected veteran SEALs were meant to be advisors again, but not like it was in 1961. This time it would be all about using a local network of Vietnamese personnel and turning them into highly mobile units to fight, capture VC, gather intelligence and spread propaganda all in VC controlled areas.

Like us SEALs, they were going to mobilize using sea, air and land transports. By being mobile, they would be able to give SEALs better information about VC supply lines so that we could sabotage them.

It was such a good idea that the Army Special Forces and the Australians wanted to get in on it—so, of course, higher authorities had to make a formal approval because additional manpower would be needed. When they finally offered me a position I didn't hesitate to accept.

After a revised plan was put in place to target VC controlled infrastructure as the main objective, the new PRU program started making headway—and it couldn't have happened at a better time because something unprecedented was about to start in South Vietnam. It would be the largest and bloodiest military operation up to that time.

The Vietnamese were planning to celebrate the most important holiday on their calendar which actually allowed both sides to have a truce. They called it the Tet festival. It was a time for lighting fireworks, traveling and visiting family—like a cross between a Thanksgiving weekend and the Fourth of July.

At this time, I was completing PRU training in Coronado under SEAL Team One when an Army Brigadier general sent an intelligence report to his field units warning them about a possible invasion during the festival.

JOINT MESSAGEFORM

SECURITY CLASSIFICATION: UNCLASSIFIED

SPACE BELOW RESERVED FOR COMMUNICATION CENTER

PRECEDENCE		TYPE MSG (Check)			ACCOUNTING SYMBOL	ORIG. OR REFERS TO	CLASSIFICATION OF REFERENCE
		BOOK	MULTI	SINGLE			
ACTION	FLASH						
INFO	FLASH		M				

FROM: CG, II FFORCEV, LBN, RVN

TO: II FFORCEV AIG 100

CG, 101ST ABN DIV, BNH, RVN

CO, 11TH ACR, LGO, RVN (REAR)

CO, 11TH ACR, LNH, RVN

CO, CO A, 5TH SFG, BNH, RVN

CO, 73D AVN CO, VTU, RVN

INFO: CG, USARV, LBN, RVN

DSA, IV CORPS, RVN

UNCLASSIFED AVFBB 10644 WEYAND SENDS

1. There are a number of positive intelligence indicators that the enemy will deliberately violate the truce by attacking friendly installations during the night of 29 Jan or the early morning hours of 30 Jan.

2. Addressees will take action to insure maximum alert posture through the TET period. Be particularly alert for enemy deception involving use of friendly vehicles or uniforms.

SPECIAL INSTRUCTIONS

DISTR:
AG
G2
G1
G3
G4
G5
Engr
Sig
Surg
HC Cmdt
SGS
PM
219th MID

DATE	TIME
29	1040Z
MONTH	YEAR
Jan	68

WRITER

SYMBOL: AVFBB

TYPED NAME AND TITLE (Signature, if required): LTC Pieper, GS, Deputy G2

PHONE: 5302 PAGE NR. 1 NR. OF PAGES 1

SECURITY CLASSIFICATION: UNCLASSIFIED

RELEASER

SIGNATURE:

TYPED (or stamped) NAME AND TITLE:
JOHN S. LEKSON
Brigadier General, GS
Chief of Staff

DD FORM 1 MAY 55 173 REPLACES DD FORM 173, 1 OCT 48, WHICH IS OBSOLETE FOR ARMY USE. U.S. GOVERNMENT PRINTING OFFICE

Military Intelligence indicators anticipating large enemy offensive maneuvers

Army intelligence was pretty accurate. The Tet Offensive began January 30th when the Viet Cong went all out to attack key targets in the South. They infiltrated and hit places near our troop stations and even our embassy in Saigon. There were over 80,000 of them. Though it was a turning point, as a military operation "Tet" really didn't do very well because they lost around 50,000 communist troops and didn't keep any captured territory. The one thing that did succeed was changing the perception of the war back home. The whole thing now made the enemy seem more resilient than expected, so the little support that was once there started to disappear.

The offensive started on a Tuesday. And by the following week I was there again, back in the mix, but this time as a PRU advisor.

The thing that kept everyone on edge was that since Tet, you really didn't know who was who among the locals. The VC had infiltrated to the point that they could have blended into any local village with sympathizers who spoke the same dialects. Even though we had been operating the "Chiêu Hồi" program, which was put together to lure VC defectors over to our side by giving them jobs if they laid down their weapons, there were no real background checks in the field. There could have been VC spies among my new team now —all I could do was just trust and pray that there weren't any and watch my own back when instinct prompted me.

There were over a hundred locals on my team, and I had to be responsible for all of them. Some would work as my interpreters, others would be point men, guards and infantrymen. But some of the finest warriors I ever worked with were the tribal Montagnard people—the ethnic minority group allied with the South Vietnamese. They mostly grew up in the jungles and lived in villages along the mountain ranges and they usually had darker skin than the Vietnamese from the cities. They had a hard time grasping concepts like communism, or democracy, but they could identify troublemakers who threatened their peaceful way of life.

The Montagnards were an oppressed people who had their own history of rebelling against the South Vietnamese government. But the South responded by trying to treat them a little better and help them reach a higher standard of living. Many of the men were used to walking around in little more than what looked like a thong around their waist. The children were often naked. But the government started giving them clothes and delivering nutritional supplements and medical supplies.

The local people never complained about being sick. For them, if you could stand up and work, you weren't sick. But when you talked about certain symptoms that were bothering them, they all had some. U.S. Army units deployed medical teams to pull aching teeth, treat tuberculosis—which a great number of them had—and give them something for their vitamin deficiencies which they all had.

They loved watching American Westerns and always seemed to identify more with the native American Indians than the cowboys. Those tribesmen actually helped my eyes open to the realization that discrimination, in some form, was more of a global issue and that you could find these types of problems anywhere you went. But some black U.S. Army soldiers were deeply disturbed saying that the Vietnamese people treated the Montagnards in the same way that blacks were being treated back home in the South—and the VC did a good job feeding into this sentiment by putting up racist oriented propaganda posters. They promised blacks special treatment if they defected from their units.

Though many Montagnards had Christian beliefs, their peaceful demeanor didn't overshadow any of their warrior capabilities. They were experts in silent weapons like homemade crossbows and darts—and when they dipped those darts in snake poison mixed with animal dung, it was usually over for any living target.

I was only an E-6 at the time. It was a little unusual for someone with that rank to be working as a PRU because he often had to advise high-ranking officers on their own ships.

The Navy had established a floating Mobile Riverine Base (MRB) using barrack ships, and barrage barges (non-self-propelled) as livable facilities for Army and Navy personnel. They could land helicopters and the whole force could move around major rivers and launch troops to attack targets. At times I had to be transported by helicopter onto the ship to discuss logistics with the commanders for offshore bombardment support and I remember thinking if they knew that I was only an E-6 they'd probably tell me to get the hell off their ship. For this reason, I took full advantage of wearing civilian clothes when advising brass hats. Thankfully, no one knew except my supreme boss, an 0-6 Marine Colonel, and an 0-6 Lieutenant Colonel that shared my quarters. The light colonel had special non-combat duties with the villagers, while my guys were commandos, and I set up a camp for them not too far from where I was.

"*The lives of my teammates and the success of our mission depend on me—my technical skill, tactical proficiency, and attention to detail.*"

—SEAL Ethos

13

THE FOREST FOR ASSASSINS

My base of operations was the swampy regions of the Rung Sat Special Zone–not unlike the muddy creeks in my hometown. The Rung Sat Special Zone was a large area of mangrove swamp located in the Mekong Delta in South Vietnam. It was approximately a thousand square km., from north to south and thirty km., from east to west. The translated meaning of the term *Rung Sat* was "the forest for assassins" and I knew instinctively that we would probably play a major part in it living up to its reputation.

As a PRU advisor I had new opportunities to build a support network of skilled combatants outside of my team. I could now work closely with the Mobile Riverine Force (MRF), which was a new unit created by the Navy to partner with the Army. The MRF used a lot of assault patrol craft and troop carriers among a few other vehicles to secure the delta region. With this combination we could fight the VC in rice paddies, canals and waterways more effectively. I even had a couple of Australians who asked to team with us. I really wasn't for working with them in the beginning because I didn't know what their capabilities were. But I eventually found out that they really knew what they were doing. Also, they brought their own Foster's Lager beer which was better than ours—and we all were glad for that.

When I got word that the senior advisor was getting frustrated with VC attacks, I suspected that he was going to devise a plan to hit them hard which would drive them out and give us an opportunity to make some captures—and I wasn't too far wrong. He initiated a series of attack operations called CORONADO XI. The mission was to conduct riverine, air, and ground search operations to search and destroy VC headquarters in the region and on nearby islands.

The Rung Sat is divided into two districts, Can Gio on the east and Quang Xu yen on the west (roughly divided by the Long Tao River). There were 20 villages and hamlets scattered throughout the Rung Sat, but the important ones were along the Long Tao and Soi Rap Rivers. There was only one road in the area, from Can Gio to Dong Hoa villages, a distance of 12 km, and it was in very poor condition and unusable.

For this reason, the only modes of transportation were

by boat or helicopter. The Rung Sat was actually 12 separate islands with no connection to the mainland where the inhabitants of several little villages survived on small fishing businesses—and this is where the problem was. Since the "Tet" offensive, VC units were now spreading out more into the islands where they could harass U.S. patrol boats in the delta with sniper fire and rocket attacks.

Driving the enemy out of hiding became the key to wiping them out, making captures, and protecting civilians. The Army realized this with their helicopter "Eagle Flight" formations. Up to a certain point they were flying their Huey gunships in squadrons of ten for search and destroy missions. The problem was this caused the enemy to hunker down—nobody was going to risk exposing themselves to ten low flying gunships with M60 machine guns. So they downsized their flight squadrons to five at a time; then they started taking on enemy fire during their flight missions and could tell us about enemy locations.

Military operations were non-stop in the region and often close to one another, but I had my own grid for organizing attacks. Constantly using scatter communications, I regularly radioed other PRU and field commanders to let them know what my attack plans were because if I didn't, my squads could have easily been wiped out by friendly fire. I'll never forget an incident when one of my interpreters was shot dead.

He was struck several times just under his neck, but I never determined whether or not the enemy had done it, or if he was a victim of friendly fire. Someone might have seen him walking close to us thinking he was VC. We had to carry his body back.

We usually patrolled the area just about every night to make captures. During the day VC units basically blended in with the locals to remain in hiding. They hid in broad daylight—but at night they were everywhere. They roamed the regions as if they owned the place and tried to take out as many ARVN and U.S. forces as they could.

After I had verified the location of VC units on an island, I contacted high command and indicated on our common chalkboard grid where I would take about 80 of my men on a shooting mission. We used a Landing Craft Medium (LCM) to take us from the main river channels to narrow streams. We approached our landing target loaded down with M16s and grenades; I had hand-selected several of the PRU operators to take their rifles with 40-millimeter grenade launcher attachments.

Two Patrol Boat Riverine (PBR) craft accompanied us for gunfire support, and they blasted the shoreline with fire until we were inserted. When the shooting stopped, there was no trace of return fire—we were being drawn in. I could see that some of my men were anxious, so I led them forward making sure they stayed abreast without anyone getting ahead.

Also, I had to always be sure that my radioman remained well behind me since they were prime targets because of their usual close proximity to their field commanders. With just one mortar round the VC could take both out and create chaos—radiomen had a very short life expectancy in the field.

When we came across a heavily weeded area—weeds so tall that they blocked all fields of vision—I called on one of my shorter men to walk the point. We covered about 100 meters while advancing when someone set off a landmine blowing dust, grass and what appeared to be body parts into the air. After that we all heard the desperate blood-curdling screams of a man in agonizing pain.

Then gun fire poured over us. We dug in and I could see tracers zinging towards us from three locations covered by heavy brush. Five men went to care for the two wounded soldiers, and we fired at will. I directed my grenade launchers to target the tracer locations. We never saw a single enemy soldier—which was common, but we returned fire for roughly eight minutes before the firing stopped—we either had them on the run, or we were being drawn in again.

I called my radioman to contact our command post and relay our location as well as my plans for advancement. I kept him close to me in case I needed to hear a response. Raising my arm to signal a slow advance we crept up to a rice field clearing. The rice paddies were flooded but not waist deep like some of the other ones we had seen. I again called one of the PRUs to walk the point suspecting that there may have been mines scattered across the paddy. When our steps were stopped by a hail of bullets plopping around us from multiple locations, we fanned out and dug into that paddy.

We were in an ambush but this time we saw the enemy along a tree line. We saw some VC fall along the edges of that rice paddy as several of my men ran their magazines dry and were reloading in a prolonged firefight. I scuttled back to cover, found my radioman and called in for a USAF C-130 "Angel of Death" for gunfire support to rake the area according to the perimeters I gave.

They must have been in the area because they arrived in no time firing from the sky. The C-130 was capable of firing nearly 6000 rounds per minute. For a while we thought we were being fired upon, but quickly saw that it was the spent shells from the C-130 falling around us—which could cause great injury when falling from that altitude. After making several sweeps through the area they provided cover until we got back to our pick up point. The risk of attacking and clearing out some of the islands was heightened because many VC would just leave the area, sneak around to a new area, blend in and recruit young men to build up another base camp to launch more attacks. We were briefed that the VC controlled about half of the islands, and they were recruiting 14 and 15 year old boys to attack us.

It was around this time when the regional commanders decided to use the Riverine Force to secure the Can Thou area where we had an airfield. VC operatives were firing rockets and mortar rounds to disrupt our base operations, so the MRF started a search and sweep response to find the

VC mortar and rocket positions. They did several riverine and ground patrols but didn't find anything until they used spotters from a helicopter squadron and saw how the VC were keeping just ahead of the ground forces. The squadron spotted them running for bunkers and called on an infantry unit nearby to take them out.

Around mid-February, the MRF did a waterborne search and clear operation on Vietnam's Cu Lao Cau island where intelligence reported 50 VC at a village—25 of which were doing their own recon work to keep ahead of us. Other VC units were used as "part-time" guerillas who could be called on for an ambush.

But we had about 44 river assault craft and 10 PBRs deployed to encircle the island. We had used some of my guys to announce by loudspeaker what was going to happen to them if they didn't surrender and report to a detainee collection center we had set up—we even dropped thousands of leaflets in the area to explain what was going to happen. After the civilians were given two hours to get to the detention areas the infantry battalions beached. They started their sweep confiscating Chicom carbines, rounds of ammo and documents.

They must have captured over a hundred male detainees and evacuated around 300 for questioning. One detainee somehow managed to escape while three of our guys were injured falling into handmade spider holes with bamboo punji stakes inside that were so sharp they could puncture right through a field boot. They eventually recovered.

High Command was pleased with how we all were working together to handle the delta region. Most of our riverine movements through the narrow waterways and canals weren't affected by enemy opposition. But they did show impressive defensive strategies around the rice patties —and they also proved that they could put up a fight for up to 24 hours. We were commended for making the best use of air, river and infantry elements blended in with ARVN units.

Back at their village the Montagnard wanted to celebrate their victory over the VC. I could see that, as an oppressed people, it was good for them to be proud of themselves—they were fighting to keep their cultural way of life. It was like going back a thousand years because that was how old some of their traditions were. With everyone gathered outside, a couple of the older men began hitting a little gong. Then some of their young men and boys formed a line balancing a wood beam over their shoulders and swayed to the beat. I remember the grin on their faces. Then young girls formed a line and did their own step in sync with graceful arm movements.

There were some symbolic movements of boys holding long sticks, pretending to be hunters with spears. Then they all rotated in a circle, keeping in step, sometimes hitting hollowed-out bamboo tubes, then holding hands. It seemed almost like a prayer and an honorary recognition ceremony rolled into one.

I was given the bronze star medal with a combat V for

my leadership as a PRU advisor in the delta region. They called my unit the most respected, active and productive elite force in the whole province, and that felt good. The Bronze Star is awarded for either heroic achievement, heroic service, or what they call meritorious achievement, or meritorious service in a combat zone—but I couldn't say exactly what I did to earn it.

There were times in my life when I knew I had to fight to earn respect. But nobody fights in a battle for that, or to win any medals; you're fighting for the guys who are with you along with the constant reminder of the ones who wouldn't make it back, and of course, you're fighting for your country. In addition to the Bronze Star, I was also awarded the Navy Commendation with combat "V", a Presidential Unit Citation, four Good Conduct awards, the Vietnamese Cross of Gallantry, and a few others. And after all that I'd seen, I still looked back and marveled at how I could have possibly completed three tours in Vietnam and participated in, as well as orchestrated, over 100 missions without ever getting shot; I was just blessed.

"We train for war and fight to win."

—SEAL Ethos

COMMANDER IN CHIEF
UNITED STATES PACIFIC FLEET

The President of the United States takes pleasure in presenting the Bronze Star Medal to

WILLIAM H. GOINES
STOREKEEPER FIRST CLASS
UNITED STATES NAVY

for service as set forth in the following:

CITATION

"For meritorious achievement in connection with operations involving conflict with an opposing foreign force while serving in the Republic of Vietnam from 7 February 1968 to 9 August 1968. As an Advisor to the Provincial Reconnaissance Unit in Ba Xuyen Province, Petty Officer GOINES trained and directed a force of over 90 combatants in paramilitary warfare designed to gather intelligence on and neutralize the Viet Cong infrastructure in the province of his responsibility. During his tour, Petty officer GOINES planned, coordinated, and directed over 100 covert intelligence and small unit reaction operations. The effect of Petty Officer GOINES' dedicated efforts with the PRU personnel and their performance on these operations were to directly influence the developement of the unit into the most productive, active, and respected elite force in the province. His devotion to his men, courage under fire while participating in highly dangerous night operations, and outstanding professionalism were in keeping with the highest traditions of the United States Naval Service."

Petty Officer GOINES is authorized to wear the Combat "V".

For the President

John J. Hyland

JOHN J. HYLAND
Admiral, U. S. Navy
Commander in Chief U. S. Pacific Fleet

Bill Goines receives the Combat V Award for successfully conducting over 100 field operations as a PRU Advisor

14

I'M NOT TAKING ORDERS FROM A 'COLORED'

Rather than complete a fourth tour in Vietnam, I was encouraged to take a temporary additional duty in the Great Lakes area. My title was UDT/SEAL Company Commander, and I had to oversee the set-up of a new pre-training program for SEAL candidates. It really was all about getting them physically ready for the Basic Underwater Demolition SEAL (BUDS) training that they would face later—if they first made it through our program. And, of course, we were interested in seeing the cream of the crop.

We put together some challenging tests: 1000-meter swims, push-ups, sit-ups, a timed four-mile run, and other minimum standard screening tests. Those that could not complete the longer, more intense tests were dropped from consideration and reclassified to other naval jobs which often meant being assigned to a ship.

Some interesting characters came through the program. A few really surprised us with their capabilities. It was still impossible to look at a man and determine whether or not he could make it through the training. Though all were strong, we had some very muscular ones who couldn't go the distance of some of the smaller guys. We had some quieter men that could outdo some of the louder more aggressive candidates, and we got an early glimpse into the personality types of some who were either already showing leadership potential or a defeatist attitude.

This experience took me back to the earlier days in '61 when I was a UDT instructor before being transferred to SEAL TEAM TWO. There was a trainee back then that stood out a little from the rest. You could see that he definitely loved being challenged. He was real gung-ho and he had ambition. He had started out as an enlistee but later became an officer and commander of SEAL TEAM 2. Was he controversial?—Yes! He had his ways about him, but I never had any problem with Richard Marcinko whom we called the "Geek." Later in his career he organized SEAL TEAM SIX which became a top counter-terrorist rescue unit.

Being an instructor sometimes gave you a peek at how SEAL teams were developing based on the caliber of the trainee. It was all about which ones were weeded out, which ones were ushered in, and which ones would need a SEAL attitude adjustment along the way. And I'd always reminded myself to uphold high standards for my men, even while I was on regular duty, and not take things too personal.

Later, as a chief, I had an interesting incident with a SEAL who respectfully asked to speak privately with me. He was a big man—massive girth and impressive height! Standing up, he towered over me as he looked down.

"Chief, may I respectfully have a word with you?" he asked.

"Sure, come on in." I took him to my office.

"Have a seat."

"No thank you sir, I'd much rather just stand if you don't mind."

"Okay, well what's going on?"

"I want to level with you chief. I'm from a little town in Georgia which is probably no bigger than a naval base. And I don't recall ever seeing a 'colored' in my town as I was growing up—except for maybe a worker who came through town every once in a while. So, uh, anyway now, I don't think I'll be able to take orders from you."

I politely extended a coffee cup to him, "Listen, can I offer you some coffee?" And he responded with politeness. I then let him explain himself more.

"With all due respect, I have never taken any order from a 'colored' and I just don't feel I'll be able to do it now!"

I glared at him and laid down the law. "You know what you're setting yourself up for, don't you? You've been through the same training I went through. You've spent a lot of time trying to build a career in the SEALs, but the way you're headed you're going to throw it all away to be put out and transferred to the Fleet where you'll still probably have to work with 'coloreds.' You know we'll have to talk with the commander—and if I know him right, you're as good as gone. But you've got to know that I won't be the one doing this to you—you'll be doing it to yourself."

I talked to him for about 30 minutes, touching a little on personal issues and essential team dynamics for the battlefield, before his demeanor changed and he broke.

"Listen, I don't want to be sent to any fleet. Please give me another chance. I stepped out here and I wanted you to know how I felt, and you've told me what the consequences would be. Can we just now leave it with that, sir? I'm going to change my ways."

I knew in my gut that he would change. He had to! And when we finally parted we both felt assured that he was going to be different. He accepted the fact that it was now 1969 and he wouldn't be able to avoid taking orders from a "colored"—as they still called us in those days. In the end he actually went on to do well by becoming a warrant officer and a very good operator.

Ironically, that year 1969 saw some progressive changes all around. They finally gave prison sentences to the guys who had killed Bobby Kennedy and Martin Luther King the year before and now little black boys were finally able to play with a new action figure that was a patriotic black superhero, "The Falcon." And of course, they sent Neil

Armstrong to the moon where he took one giant leap for all of mankind.

"In the worst of conditions, the legacy of my teammates steadies my resolve and silently guides my every deed."

—SEAL Ethos

15

FROM MASTER CHIEF TO BECOMING "UNCLE BILLY"

The Navy was also onto something new in 1969 which would eventually afford me an opportunity to excel again on a special team like I hadn't in years. But while the Navy was putting it together, I had some things of my own that I wanted to achieve.

I transferred over to Naval Special Warfare Group TWO as a Senior Chief to enhance my promotion opportunities. I worked in Research Development Test and Evaluation, (RDT&E), which was a great job requiring me to travel a lot and acquire improved boats, parachutes, or whatever new things SEALs would need. But my heart was really set on becoming a Master Chief Petty Officer, so I applied for consideration.

Back then it was competitive to move up in ranks. The Navy didn't give tests to achieve a superior status; you were evaluated based on your specialties and it got a little intense. You had to be a good fit. Your whole history with SEALs was under a microscope for review. At this point I simply prayed and hoped for the best—though I started to have doubts that my expectations might have been too high. But after the panel of officers evaluated me, I was told they gave an affirmative recommendation. I was elated!

Being promoted to Master Chief was like the last piece of a puzzle finally being laid in place. Once promoted, I was selected to become the Command Master Chief for all the SEALs on the East Coast and that was truly an honor. I was now the senior enlisted person working between the commanding officer at Naval Special Warfare Group TWO and all enlisted personnel throughout all of the Group TWO subordinate commands. My job was to assist the CO with issues involving training, morale, discipline, and overall, the quality of life for all our enlisted men and women. What I consider to be my crowning non-combat operational achievement, however, was when I became a member and leader of the east coast "Chuting Stars" that was one of the Navy's two parachute demonstration teams. Men from the west coast UDT and SEAL Teams had previously organized a demonstration team called the "Leap Frogs."

Both teams went through several name changes since their beginning in '69, but both were eventually funded by the Navy Recruiting Command to perform throughout the country. This later actually evolved into a formal parachute team that today continues to perform year-round as the "Leap Frogs."

The jump teams were composed primarily of SEALs but also included Special Warfare Combatant Craft Crewmen (SWCC), Explosive Ordnance Technicians (EOD) and crew support personnel. We were like a Dream Team of Navy jumpers, and it was exhilarating—an experience beyond words.

But at the same time, we had to be able to lift heavy gear and maneuver ourselves against wind resistance at speeds up to 120 mph, so we had to stay in good shape and often think fast. Criss-crossing the skies leaving colored trails of smoke, we performed gravity-defying air stunts throughout the whole country to demonstrate our exceptional skills and promote Navy recruiting.

Because we were on a show schedule everything had to be timed; how long we had to stay in the air to do stunts and how long they wanted us to stay on the ground to interact with the fans. These were always the first two questions that required an answer, so we often did a practice jump to time ourselves and test the drop zone. When we actually jumped from high altitudes and began to descend in stadiums and fields, we could always hear the distant cheers, screams and thunder of applause—and we knew we were their heroes.

Bill Goines as team leader for the Chuting Stars

I could only imagine how some of the children felt tracking us through the skies overhead, sometimes with binoculars, and watching us land on their athletic fields. We must have been larger than life, and then we reached out to shake their hands. Captivating the minds of children was becoming extra special to me at this time.

Back home I found increasing satisfaction in my expanding role as "Uncle Billy." When my wife and I married we understood that my six-month rotating deployment schedule would create a hardship for raising children in the way we saw fit—and then there was the real possibility of me never coming back. But ironically, I had a nephew who also had to travel a great deal for his career in a popular rhythm and blues band. Gregory Seay was a drummer for the Isley Brothers and often had to go on tour.

Since his daughter, my great niece Cherise, needed more paternal support in her life, I (*when I was available*) and her paternal grandfather, who adopted her, helped shepherd this little one until she was able to move from Ohio and attend Hampton University in Virginia—a historical black research university not far from us.

It felt good dropping her off at college and hanging around just to chat. We were proud of her. Somehow she thought I was funny, so it was always easy to make her laugh. She became my little girl.

Uncle "Billy" with little Cherise

There was also "my little boy" Gene, my wife's nephew whose father had died. Anytime there seemed to be a child-rearing concern for Gene, they would send him to see me. My wife knew when to remove herself from the room to allow us to talk in private. I began to understand more precisely that I wasn't simply dealing with a little child—but a boy who was going to necessarily transition one day to manhood. I tried to pour into Gene some of the life lessons I had learned in SEALs—the chief one being that he needed to let go of any defeatist attitudes in order to achieve desirable goals. He never wanted to disappoint me and became like a son. On one occasion I had to return to base and retrieve something I had left in a locker, and I had Gene with me. We SEALs had our own protocol when escorting family members on base and they must have heard me coming with Gene.

"Kid on deck!" someone shouted, (it might have been Rudy Boesch whose appearances on the *Survivor* TV series would later become one of the few programs I'd continually watch) which meant that all poker playing cards, cigars and any other civilian contraband had to be covered up quickly. We had to maintain a positive image. I became a door to a world of adventure that little Gene could escape through when he needed it. Sometimes he would make pup tent structures from some of the old and no longer usable parachutes I'd bring back from the team. He would be the first in the family to graduate from college and he later became successful working in public education.

Before retiring, I was transferred to SEAL Team 4 after my TAD assignment with the Chuting Stars. After retiring I became the Chief of Police for the Portsmouth, Virginia public school district. But looking back on my life with the SEALs—retiring after thirty-two years—has been like turning the pages of a history book whose images have me in the foreground against a background of different faces—some are black, some are white, some are brown—and some are camouflaged. But the background represents honor, struggle, accomplishments, happiness, anger, sadness and sacrifice. It is a story not only that I've lived, but one that's still being written in the lives of my family, buddies, brethren and any citizen of this great country that dares to set goals by which to live and die.

Bill's residential hallway colorfully decorated in a timeline with the photographed faces of family, friends and loved ones

ABOUT THE AUTHOR

Rodney Walker has taught U.S History over ten years. He is also an adjunct professor of Political Science and Middle Eastern studies. Walker specializes in historic novels and has had his first historical novel, *Destiny's Spear*, represented at a London Book Fair exhibit.

He attended Briar Cliff University in Sioux City, Iowa where he earned a Bachelor's degree in Mass Communication and contributed to the campus newspaper as a staff member specializing in news features and creative writing assignments. He also interned in London, England with BBC radio for local "Radio London" broadcasts and later attended Troy University where he attained an MS in International Relations.

Walker spent several years living in North Africa where he taught English and researched "Operation Torch", the first amphibious landing of World War II employing Navy Scout and Raider units, forerunners to the Navy SEALs, in their first underwater mission.

Some of his latest achievements include producing a cable television program entitled "God's Grace on the Battlefield" featuring the personal testimonies of combat veterans who attributed their survival to miraculous events.

Walker currently teaches World History and U.S History for a public school district in Virginia.He enjoys spending time with his family, traveling and writing meaningful stories that convey life lessons.

You can find Rodney's website here:
rodneywalkerbooks.com

www.ingramcontent.com/pod-product-compliance
Ingram Content Group UK Ltd.
Pitfield, Milton Keynes, MK11 3LW, UK
UKRC031052310726
14090UKWH00028B/478

9798218987985